Teaching Women to Shoot

A Law Enforcement Instructor's Guide

Vicki Farnam and Diane Nicholl

Teaching Women to Shoot: A Law Enforcement Instructor's Guide
by Vicki Farnam and Diane Nicholl

For information, address:
DTI Publications, Inc.
PO Box 18746
Boulder, CO 80308-1746

ISBN: 0-9659422-3-6

Cover photo of Karen Melcher by John and Jenny Higgs.
Cover design by Shasti O'Leary Soudant
www.shasti.com

Warning and Disclaimer
This book is sold as is, without warranty of any kind, either express or implied. While every precaution has been taken in the preparation of this book, the authors and DTI Publications, Inc assume no responsibility for errors or omissions. Neither the authors nor DTI Publications, Inc shall have any liability to any person or entity with respect to any loss or damage caused or alleged to be caused directly or indirectly by the instruction contained in this book. It is further stated that neither the author nor DTI Publications, Inc assumes any responsibility for the use or misuse of the information or instructions contained herein.

Dedication

To John and Kirk

Acknowledgments

So many people have encouraged me to write this book or helped in my own learning process and I would like to thank them all. The following list undoubtedly is lacking in a name or two. If I have missed you, please let me hear about it! I know I would never have started writing had not my husband, John, kept telling me that this information had to be put on paper. He didn't want to hear how difficult it was or how I would rather teach than write. He just said it had to be done. John was echoed by our good friend, Steve Hoch, who with the usual tenacity of an attorney, would not let go of the idea.

Once the words were out of my mouth to my soon-to-be co-author, Diane Nicholl, the process began. It certainly could not have been done without Diane's cool and logical assessment of every hurdle we had to cross, her unfailing enthusiasm for the project, and her experience based knowledge of the subject. Thank goodness for her patience and Kirk's as well because we started this project so very long ago!

A special thanks to Wesley Garner. Wes is a veteran educator and shooter who spent hours and hours discussing educational philosophy and brain differences with me. Those discussions were the beginning of the curriculum I have used for instructor classes. And to Manny Kapelsohn who coerced me into writing my first article about guns which were too big for female officers.

Thanks to those people who have instructed me as I experienced all the same struggles that are discussed in the text. Lance Weber, one of my early instructors who is now deceased, was second only to John in encouraging me to stand in front of a group and teach. The Ohio Gang, as we fondly call them, Keith Brown, Gordon and SuAnn Cook, Bill DeWeese, Andy Evans, are dedicated officers who take their training very seriously. Years ago they invited me to be a participant in their annual training session they hold with John. They are the best group of instructors with whom anyone could hope to train. Not only did I polish my shooting skills by training with them but instructing skills too as I watched them work with students. And, it is from them that I learned of the honor of the regiment.

Thanks to those at IALEFI who have been so supportive of this material, Frank Repass, Bob Bossey and Kim Bossey, all the board members and general members who have attended classes. Thanks to Tom Walker and Dave McElhiney for teaching the first IALEFI class with me.

Thanks to Skip Gochenour for encouraging me and other women to participate at the NTI and for all the lessons learned there. Thanks to those people who have specifically promoted women's classes, Joe Smolarz, Joe Myers, Ralph Ball, Mark Guzy, Dan Abbott, Rick Benson and Marion Ratliff.

Thanks to those men who have so patiently instructed women's classes with me. Bob Berry, Scott Camp, Steve Camp, Mike Bradford, Billy Stowers, Dennis Tobin, Rick Campbell, Stan Heckrodt, Jack Branson, Steve Van Mol, Jack Richard, Marc Richard. To those who believe that women need equipment that is made specifically for them:Warren Bard, Greg Garrett, Mitch Rosen, Dave Elderton, Dick Davis and Pete Pi.

Thanks to those women who are competent shooters and who have reached out to other women: Ann Berry, Dr. Barbara Sutton, Linda Zerwin, Gila May-Hayes, and Barry Kapelsohn, Ann Persons, Jen Coy, Toni Camp, Paige Smolarz, Kristin Peterson and Wendi Lankister.

Thanks to Sergeant Sandy Nelson of the Boulder Sheriff's Department, Karen Melcher, Ellen Frohsinn and everyone else who helped with our photos but wish to remain anonymous.

Thanks to Judy Galbraith and Ann Richard for gently never letting me forget that this book had to be done. To all those women who have been students and have repeatedly verified the contents of this book.

Thanks to Kirk Webb and Frank Pytko, editors extraordinaire, for reading and commenting on this manuscript.

Last but not least, thanks to all our family and friends for their patience and understanding as well as help and encouragement.

About the Authors

Vicki Farnam has been instructing with her husband, John Farnam, since 1986. She also independently teaches classes for women and classes for instructors, both law enforcement and non-law enforcement. Prior to becoming a firearms instructor she used her degree in history and education in the field of historical interpretation.

Diane Nicholl grew up where guns were common place. She has enjoyed shooting from the time she was ten years old and would go plinking with a .22 single shot rifle. She worked in the field of neurophysiology for 15 years before finding that she could no longer balance research and teaching firearms classes. In 1996, she started her own business, DTI Publications, Inc. where she teaches firearms courses and publishes firearms training books. She is an NRA Training Counselor.

Vicki Farnam and Diane Nicholl welcome your comments or questions. Please contact them at www.DTIPubs.com.

Table of Contents

A Typical Scenario

In a department with 100 officers, over half have a record of marginally passing weapons qualification. Almost all of the women officers take two or more attempts to pass. Those struggling to qualify only go to the range when it is mandatory. At least two new recruits grumble about having to carry a gun. A male range officer complains that the female officers "cry like rats eating onions" and a female officer is threatening to file a hostile work environment complaint about conditions at the range.

From Vicki Farnam

The first call came from the head firearms instructor with a major southern California city. He had a female officer who was repeatedly failing her qualification tests. Then a chief of police in Wyoming called. His department had five women who needed their confidence boosted. An instructor for a regional state academy in Colorado, (one of my own mentors), was next. He was totally puzzled that as successful as he had been for years at instructing men, he found that as women began attending, they were failing miserably. He called to ask if I thought his skill as an instructor was slipping or was there some light I could shed for him on this dilemma.

By the time these calls started coming in I had been teaching with my husband John for a number of years. In our classes I taught far more men than women. But, by reviewing what I had observed of the women who had been in training classes, and thinking back on how I had learned, I reached a fundamental conclusion to this curriculum. Women do far better in firearms instruction when they are given more detailed information and more time to absorb that information than the details and time required by the average male receiving the same instruction.

Several years ago I had the very good fortune to meet Diane Nicholl. She had been teaching firearms for many years at her local gun club. She instructed both women and men but had indeed found that the progress made by women did not quite match that made by men in the same class. After discussing this situation at length, we began our search for answers.

We knew women certainly could learn to shoot, and to shoot well. We each had confidence in our own abilities and we both knew other women who were competent. So how had we, and those others we knew, managed to achieve success, but other women, especially women in law enforcement, were failing? Women who were being trained by experienced, professional, full time law enforcement instructors. Instructors who had records to prove their success with countless male officers but only a very, very small number of successful female officers, if any at all.

One day Diane was approached by three local female law enforcement officers who needed to learn how to shoot so that they could pass their department's qualification test. I say "needed to learn how" because with their repeated qualification failures, they were at risk of having their guns taken away from them by the department for which they worked. We both spent time on the range with these women. I am pleased to say that they did learn.

After that experience, we decided that we needed to seek out other women in law enforcement and find out if they needed, or wanted, help also. And they did!

What we learned in that first class, what we learned in subsequent classes for female officers, and what I learned as I asked questions of female officers I worked with from one end of the country to the other, is the basis of what we have used to create this book. But it became obvious that we had to approach this problem from both sides. We also started offering classes to male instructors to share what we had learned from the female officers' classes. When we took this information to male instructors, they looked at us as though we were crazy! How could women think like that? How could they fail to learn? And yet these same male instructors knew there was a problem with teaching female officers to shoot competently.

So we taught and we learned, and we read and we learned, we asked questions and we learned and we taught some more. Some instructors have eagerly absorbed this information. Others have been skeptical, and some have been downright hostile. What we are looking to do is to give information to any instructor who is looking for it. You be the judge as to how successful it is for you and your students.

From Diane Nicholl

This book is the distillation of what we have found to improve the shooting skills of women. The teaching techniques we present have proven successful for novice as well as more experienced shooters. Our approach is to teach students a core technique that allows them to understand what it takes physically and mentally to consistently hit the target. Ideally, the student will be able to tell what she has done to cause her to miss the target and know how to correct her problem.

I was motivated to write this book because I found most of the female officers I work with have never learned the fundamentals of shooting. They do not understand why they cannot accurately hit the target. I have also heard from firearms instructors who feel like they have hit a brick wall trying to get female officers qualified.

Our goal for this book is to present information that instructors and students can use to help them shoot to the best of their ability. We cannot do this without acknowledging that there is a difference in how women and men learn shooting skills.

It is important to understand that we are discussing the "average" woman and the "average" man. There will always be exceptions. For example, there are women who can run a mile in just over four minutes and there are men who struggle to finish in eight minutes. In general, the "average" man will run a mile in less time than the "average" woman. This does not make one gender superior to the other, it is just the way our bodies work.

Part I
Gender Differences

Chapter 1
Introduction

A female deputy sheriff in the 1950's was often handed a uniform, a revolver and a badge. She might go to the range once a year to fire her gun but would not be required to shoot a weapons qualification course. During her career, she would receive little formal firearms training. Today every woman who enters the field of law enforcement receives firearms instruction while attending an academy. Yet this training does not seem to be working well for many female recruits. In agencies across the nation, women are still more likely than men to fail their weapons qualifications and are more likely to be receiving remedial firearms training.

Extensive investigation of this problem leads us to conclude that men and women learn shooting skills in different ways. Typically women learn best when the fundamentals of shooting are broken down into small segments and there is time to master each part before new material is presented. In other words, women want detailed instruction and adequate time to practice a new skill. Men typically do not need such detailed explanations. This fact helps to explain why some of the methods instructors have used successfully with male students do not work as well for female students.

We believe an increase in the number of struggling shooters may also be related to the growing percentage of male and female recruits entering law enforcement with no prior experience with firearms. Instructors accustomed to teaching students who are familiar with firearms may not realize how many new recruits have never touched a gun or set foot on a firing range. These students are often too self-conscious to ask questions and they leave the academy without fully understanding the fundamentals of shooting. We work with both male and female officers from across the country who do not fully understand the relationship between their eye, the rear sight, front sight and where the bullet strikes the target.

Over the years, we have come to understand the frustrations of both the firearms instructors and the officers who are struggling with their firearms skills. The good news is - It does not have to be this way! The bad news is - There is no instant cure. The transformation from a struggling shooter to a competent shooter does not happen overnight. We know that time on the range is a precious commodity so our goal is to help instructors learn how to make the most of each training session.

An instructor who excels is one who is determined to meet the needs of her students. She is continually searching for ways to improve her own skill and for new teaching "tools." Teaching a struggling shooter how to perfect her skill is hard work and often takes every ounce of patience an instructor has. The pay off is seeing a shooter draw her weapon and hit the center of the target without giving a second thought to the technique that now comes naturally.

Chapter 2
Male and Female Brains

While almost everyone is aware of the obvious anatomical differences between men and women, a surprising number of people do not realize how much difference there is between the male and female brains. The male and female pattern of brain organization has advantages and disadvantages for both sexes. How our brain is designed to handle a specific activity is what allows us to be better at some tasks and have difficulty with others. Knowing that male and female brains process information in different ways, which result in different perceptions, priorities and behaviors will help you as a firearms trainer.

The most recent research shows there are a greater number of connections between the two sides of a female brain than there are in a male brain. This means more information is being exchanged between the left and right sides of the female brain. This arrangement allows the average woman to perform multiple tasks while the average man concentrates on one specific task at a time.

The female brain is also organized to respond more sensitively to sensory stimuli. For example, women have better hearing sensitivity than men which makes it easy to notice small changes in volume of sound, especially in regards to someone's tone of voice. This helps explain why women are usually better than men at recognizing the emotional nuances in voice, gesture and facial expression. This is not to say that a woman's interpretations are always correct.

It may be that women cry more often than men because they are receiving more emotional input, strongly reacting to it and expressing it with greater intensity. Usually if a man were in a similar situation, he may not have actually registered the hurt or insult, either at all or to the same degree that a woman might. In other words, it literally means less to him. However when a man does cry, it is usually an indication that something is badly or deeply wrong.

The male brain is organized in such a way that it gives men an edge in dealing with mechanical devices such as firearms or motor vehicles. A man can more easily put together an object by looking at a diagram than a woman can. When presented with the task of rearranging tables in a classroom from rows into a smaller square inside a larger square, a group of men will typically start by moving the tables. Women given the same task will almost always discuss how they will proceed before moving the tables.

Also it seems men have a greater desire for knowledge and skill at managing the mechanical world than women do. When a man is presented with a new firearm, he usually does not hesitate before he picks it up and tries to figure out how it works. A woman will usually want to know what each button or lever does before she attempts to handle the gun.

Although women may not be as interested in the mechanical details of their firearms, they do want to feel confident that they know how their gun functions and how to properly maintain it. They usually have little desire to memorize all the different models offered by a particular gun manufacturer. Women in general treat their firearms as a utilitarian piece of equipment.

Men more often than not seek to customize their firearms. They are more likely to read gun magazines, attend gun shows, competitions and keep up with the newest innovations in firearms. Men who are interested in firearms may be very knowledgeable regarding the various features offered by several manufacturers.

Chapter 3
Gender Differences in Spatial and Verbal Skills

Men have successfully taught other men firearms skills for generations. They developed techniques to allow them to do this effectively and efficiently. As more women enter law enforcement, some instructors find female students have more difficulty learning to shoot accurately.

Our experience teaches us there is a difference in how some men and women learn firearms skills. Basically, our brains are not alike. Two areas in which men and women differ are their spatial and verbal skills. A better understanding of these two areas helps the instructor develop effective teaching techniques to meet the needs of both male and female students.

Here is an example of how each gender perceives and understands spatial relationships.

Debra wants to rearrange the living room furniture. Jim tells her the sofa will not fit in the space where she wants to move it. She finds this hard to believe because the mental picture she has created shows that the sofa will fit. Jim agrees to help her move the sofa and she is surprised when the sofa cannot be squeezed into place.

Jim's spatial skill allowed him to mentally compare the size of the sofa and the size of the space. He does not understand why Debra cannot see the outcome without having to move the sofa. She does not understand how he can tell "just by looking" that the sofa will not fit.

Chapter 4
Spatial Relationships and Spatial Skills

We define spatial relationship as the ability to picture objects, their shape, position, proportion and their relationship to one another in the mind's eye. Spatial skills use spatial relationships to accomplish a particular goal, i.e. accurately hitting the target. It is crucial that students understand the spatial relationship between the front sight, rear sight, their eye, the trigger, the target and the hole in the target. They must learn that wherever the front sight is pointed when the bullet leaves the muzzle, is where the bullet will hit the target.

In general, men have more highly developed spatial abilities than women. Again we are talking about "average" because there are women with highly developed spatial abilities and there are men with poor spatial abilities. This means most men need little explanation about the relationship between the front sight, rear sight, their eye, the trigger, the target and the hole in the target. They can quickly visualize the reason the sights must be aligned, and they understand that this alignment results in hitting the target in the desired spot. Many male instructors spend little time explaining this spatial relationship because it seems like common sense to them; they think everyone should just understand.

A few years ago, we were teaching a group of male law enforcement instructors. After we explained why a female student might need a detailed description of the relationship between her eye, the front sight, rear sight and the hole in the target, one instructor pounded his desk and exclaimed, "But that's just common sense, everybody knows that!" He had a hard time accepting that everyone does not intuitively understand this spatial relationship.

Most women hear the words but fail to make the specific spatial connection between the rear sight, front sight, eye, the trigger, the target and the hole in the target. They might successfully hit the target the first few times because they are following explicit instructions. Their success may rapidly fade when they start adding movement to the gun by mashing the trigger or anticipating recoil. Combine this with their lack of understanding of the firearm's spatial relationships and the result is a shooter who has no idea why they hit or miss the target.

Male and female shooters who do understand the spatial relationship necessary to accurately hit the target are not always successful either. They add movement to the gun by jerking the trigger or flinching. These shooters know what should happen if they align their sights and carefully press the trigger, however they are not aware of how they add movement to the gun.

One experience that convinced us women in general do not intuitively understand the spatial relationships of shooting occurred during a class for female law enforcement officers. These women represented different agencies and some had been in law enforcement between ten and fifteen years. To confirm that they understood sight picture and sight alignment, we asked them to place an X on the target to show where they put their front sight. Imagine our surprise when *none* of them put an X in the center of the target! Most placed the mark high and to the right of the center of the target.

It is hard to believe that a shooter would place her front sight anywhere on the target other than where she wants the round to hit. This drawing shows where right-handed officers typically put their sights in order to hit the center of the target. Left-handed shooters put their front sight high and to the left in order to hit the center of the target. One officer explained how she put her front sight in one position (not the center of the target) when she was at seven yards and moved her front sight to a different position (again not the center of the target) when she was at fifteen yards.

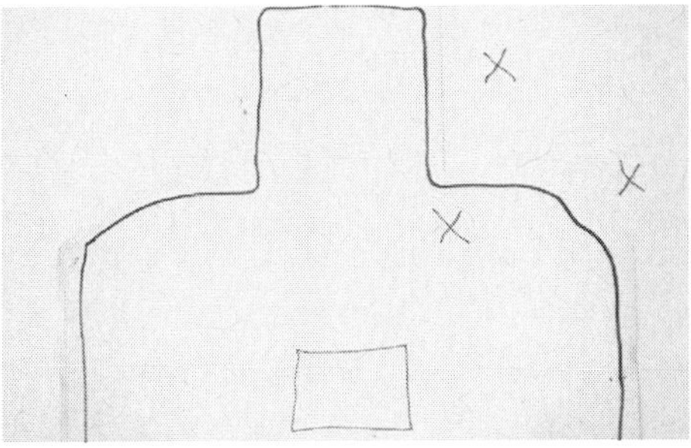

This illustration shows the areas where the students were most likely to place their front sight if they wanted to hit in the center of the target.

These officers could not explain why a hole would sometimes appear in the center of the target if they placed their front sight to the right and higher than the center. They did not understand that the way they pressed the trigger caused the front sight to move so they did not hit the target where they intended nor where they had aimed.

Once we found that none of the officers placed their front sight in the middle of the target, we explained the spatial relationship between the shooter's eye, rear sight, front sight, trigger press and where a hole would appear in the target. Next we went over in detail how to grip the gun, align the sights and press the trigger. We explained how to minimize movement of the sights and how they must be mentally aware of what their bodies are doing. We stressed how they must continually confirm that the front sight is aligned with the rear sight as they press the trigger.

This class was not conducted at the range and we could only do dry fire drills. However, all their range officers reported that the women who attended our class had greatly improved their accuracy. The officers finally understood what they needed to do to accurately hit the target and how to make corrections when they missed.

We have found numerous female officers across the nation have figured out how to "solve" their shooting problem by studying their target. If they see that most of the hits are low and to the left, they move their front sight high and to the right in hopes that the holes move to the center of the target. Most officers admitted that even though some hits were in the center, quite a few still missed the target. They could not explain to us what caused them to miss. They just knew that they had the best chance of hitting the middle of the target if they placed their front sight somewhere above and to the right of where they wanted to hit. Officers who are consistent in how they add movement to the gun will usually pass their qualification.

In some cases, the struggling shooter had been told by fellow officers or instructors to move where she aimed or placed her front sight (not to place it in the center of the target). Correcting one error by committing another error will never consistently solve the problem.

> *Kevin, a deputy sheriff, shared a conversation he had with one of his female officers. She told him she did not place her sights in the middle of the target if that is where she wanted her hits to be. She put them up near the left ear on the qualification target. Another instructor had told her to do that as a cure for flinching. Kevin said, "Well I nearly dropped my teeth. I have known this instructor for 15 years and I do not agree with him on several things, but I never thought he would do something that lazy. Guess I'm the dummy."*

The practice of placing the front sight on an area of the target other than the place you want to hit is not exclusive to women officers. For example, two officers from a federal agency came to the range - the woman had been referred for remedial training and the man just wanted some extra practice. Both officers started firing from seven yards then moved to fifteen yards shooting at paper targets.

The officer who was there to practice had a very consistent group at both distances so he switched to the steel plate rack. The other officer had more scatter at fifteen yards and continued working on paper targets. What happened next really surprised us. We did not watch the officer shooting the steel plate rack, but could hear what was going on. The officer fired several shots before he finally hit a plate. This pattern continued for all six plates. How could he miss the plate when he had such a good group on the paper target?

He was honest enough to tell us that when he shot the paper targets, he placed his front sight high and to the right of the center of the target. Basically he solved his shooting problem by moving where he pointed the sights. He was so used to shooting at paper targets that he could easily figure out just where to put the sights to make center-of-mass hits. When he moved to the steel plates, he did not have a reference point to place his sight and of course missed the target. This officer had no trouble passing his qualifications. The firearms instructors at his agency had no idea he had failed to master the skills of sight alignment and trigger control.

An extreme example of the lack of understanding of spatial relationships occurred during a practice shoot using a barricade. Officers were told to shoot from the right side of the barricade, then the left side. One female officer held her gun on the right side of the barricade and moved her head to look past the left side. She then reversed the gun and her head position. The range officer ask her if she had not been told that she had to hold the gun so that her eye was behind the sights. After he explained the proper sight picture and alignment, she asked, "How does the bullet know where to go?"

Struggling shooters are told over and over that they are jerking the trigger and that is making them miss. They may hear the words, "line up your sights and press the trigger" and yet they do not realize that they need to keep the front sight steady *while* they press the trigger. They may take the verbal instruction literally and think that lining up the sights and pressing the trigger are two separate steps. This means that they line up the sights and fail to continue to focus on the front sight as they press the trigger. What is needed is an explanation of how to *simultaneously* monitor the front sight and press the trigger. The shooter may need to be reminded that wherever the front sight is on the target when the bullet leaves the muzzle is where the bullet will hit the target.

Chapter 5
Verbal skills

We define verbal skills to include the use of language for communication. In general, women have highly developed verbal skills. The average female brain has more connections between the left and right hemisphere than the male brain. Research shows women use both the left and right hemispheres for language while men use only the left hemisphere.

It is a well-documented fact that men and women have very different styles of communication. Men often use a single word to convey a concept. For example when a man goes on an outing for business or recreation and returns home, his wife will usually ask, "How was your trip?" The typical male response sums up his experience in one word. No matter what the circumstances were - good, lousy or okay - the experience is summed up in one word. The details seem insignificant because to a male, one word says it all.

When a woman is asked, "how was your trip?" she usually gives a day-by-day description. She talks about the details in order to explain what made the trip good or bad. Detailed explanations are common when women talk with other women.

Men can usually go from point A to point B with a minimum of instruction. Women need all the steps in between - A1 thru A10 - that lead to point B. In other words, women learn more quickly when information is presented in detail and in an orderly sequence. Men typically do not need such detailed explanations. In fact if the instructor spends more time providing detailed instructions, the male students may become bored and perhaps stop paying attention.

The bottom line is that women use an abundance of details when they describe something. Women also want detailed descriptions when they are learning. Men do not use a lot of words to describe something and usually do not want a detailed description when they are learning. Of course there are exceptions.

> *Vicki taught a firearms class that included two rocket scientists. After her presentation about teaching methods for women, one scientist approached her. He stood right in her face and said, "Now I know why I have never learned anything from a female instructor. They drown me in minutiae!"*
>
> *What he was actually saying confirms the flip side of the coin. Women find detail important in both their communication to others as well as depending upon it when listening to and learning from someone else. Men are bored by an emphasis on detail.*
>
> *The second scientist explained that the first scientist was not trying to hurt her feelings!*

Literal Listening

We include listening as part of verbal skills. Students who allow themselves to be distracted or daydream often miss important parts of lectures or range commands. Listening skills include being alert, staying focused on what is being said and avoiding distractions.

Women tend to be very literal in their listening. They will often do "exactly" as told. They may not interpret what the instructor says and will therefore do exactly what they heard the instructor say. For example, when told to align their sights and press the trigger, some women may think that the instruction is a two-part process and perform each one independent of the other rather than doing both simultaneously. If they think of the instruction as a two-part process, they may be focused on the target rather than the front sight. They miss the target and the instructor tells them to "line up your sights and press the trigger." The shooter thinks she is doing exactly that but she continues to miss the target and does not understand why. To correct this problem, the instructor needs to provide more detailed instruction. The shooter needs to understand that she must simultaneously keep her eye focused on the front sight, keep it aligned with the rear sight and press the trigger straight to the rear.

Another difference we find is that women learn more when firearms information is presented in small segments, in an orderly sequence and they are given time for numerous repetitions before moving on to the next segment. Most women want to master one step before they start the next. If they do not have time to absorb the information, they may still be thinking about a previous segment while a new one is discussed. As a result, they fall behind and are lost. Men on the other hand want the big picture and can move rapidly from concept to concept.

Chapter 6
Learning = Time + Technique

We look at learning as an equation. If there is an unlimited amount of time for a class, students may learn in spite of marginal teaching techniques. However, if there is a limited amount of time for a class, the instructor had best use an efficient teaching technique.

As mentioned in the previous chapter on verbal skills, women tend to require a more detailed, step-by-step explanation. This needs to be combined with small blocks of information and more time to relate the new information with the previous instruction.

There is no perfect solution to this problem. An instructor must try to balance the amount of detail and repetition during the class. Demonstrations and/or illustrations can be used to reinforce the verbal descriptions of the proper grip, stance and sight alignment and will help the student form a mental image of how she should stand and move. Another way to help is to provide very detailed material for the students so they can continue to learn outside the classroom. If possible, set aside a time before or after class for additional help with opportunities for further repetition of skills and/or demonstrations by the instructional staff.

The dilemma facing a firearms instructor is how to best meet the needs of both male and female students. Male students can easily become bored with too much detail and repetition. Yet we know from experience that an effective teaching technique for women includes additional time for absorbing information and practicing skills. It has been demonstrated over and over that lack of adequate instructional time coupled with a lack of detailed information has a negative affect on the overall learning of gun handling skills and accuracy. The result is poor qualification scores.

In an experiment at a law enforcement academy, female students were invited to participate in an additional day of instruction at the range before the regular classes began. Instructors presented the same material that would be taught on the first day of class. The difference being they used greater detail when giving instruction and provided more time for the students to ask questions and to repeat procedures such as locking the slide to the rear, loading and unloading etc.

The instructors found that the women asked more questions than they normally would have in a mixed gender class. They also found the women were better able to work through their frustration at learning to physically operate the gun. Another important discovery came when the groups were recombined. The women had no difficulty keeping up with the pace of the class. The women's progress through the rest of the firearms sections was significantly improved compared to previous years.

Chapter 7
Learning

Good shooting is a combination of physical and mental processes. Development of shooting skill comes from understanding what one is doing. Many female shooters we work with have never really learned the fundamentals of shooting. As a result, they do not understand what it feels like (physically and mentally) to consistently make good shots. In other words, they do not know what they are doing incorrectly nor do they know what they need to do to shoot accurately.

A female shooter may do very well and improve during a training session where she has one-on-one instruction, then revert to being mediocre the next time she goes to the range and has to perform on her own. In most cases, she is relying on the instructor to solve her shooting problem for her by telling her what to do. She does not really understand why she hits or misses the target. She may tell you she is "holding the front sight steady and pressing the trigger" yet she may not comprehend what these words mean. Our assumption of a new or struggling shooter's knowledge and understanding of the shooting fundamentals is not always correct.

Another factor to be considered is the shooter may not have a disciplined routine to follow. Many officers tell us they are given different instructions each time they shoot. If instructors use a systematic approach that allows their officers to learn a specific skill well, these officers will always have that to fall back on when things go wrong.

As the shooter becomes more practiced in the fundamentals of shooting, she will develop more control and therefore spend less time consciously thinking about her stance, grip, sight alignment, trigger press and follow through; in other words, all those details. With the understanding of what it takes to make a good shot, she no longer has to think about what she ought to do. She now does it without having to consciously focus on it.

Before a shooter reaches this level of skill, she requires feedback which allows her to understand what she must do to make a good shot. The point is to get her to practice the fundamentals until they are as perfect as she can make them. We encourage the new or struggling shooter to learn how to do each step well and consistently. For example, reloading and holstering the firearm should be done with confidence and economy of motion. We do not allow sloppy or unsafe gunhandling at any time.

We cannot overemphasize the importance of a shooter understanding as precisely as possible what she needs to do physically and mentally to make an accurate shot. A reliable and simple core technique that is understood and practiced along with a positive attitude, will improve the novice and struggling shooters' performance.

Basically we see four levels of awareness in the students with whom we work.

Unconscious Incompetence

This refers to a person who does not know that she cannot accurately fire a gun. For example, the recruit who has never handled a firearm, set foot on a firing range or talked with anyone who shoots. She has no idea what it takes to accurately hit a target.

Conscious Incompetence

At this stage, the novice or struggling shooter is aware that she does not know enough to accurately hit a target. With good instruction, she will start to understand the physical and mental skills necessary to shoot well. Her coordination and timing will be awkward until muscle memory starts to develop.

Conscious Competence

As muscle memory develops and the shooter has some grasp of the fundamentals, she will not have to focus on each step. She will still need to think about what she is doing.

Unconscious Competence

With continued practice, the shooter will become more confident of her physical skills and will perform them automatically. For example, when presented with a threat, the shooter will quickly and smoothly draw her gun and align the sights without having to think about it.

Assumption of Knowledge

Here is an example of how easy it is to assume that an officer knows more than she really does about firearms. When an officer we had been working with moved to a new agency, she asked for range time to become familiar with the Glock pistol. We explained that the Glock is a more simple design than the Beretta she had been using as it does not have a decocking lever. She was asked to load her gun. After she inserted the magazine, she asked if she had to pull the slide back and let it go to load a round as she had done with her other pistol. Her question made us realize that even though she had been carrying an autoloading pistol for over eight years she did not fully understand how they worked. We now make it a habit to confirm that the shooter understands how her firearm works.

Chapter 8
Launch Platform

The "Launch Platform" is a technique used when the gun is at eye level and the trigger finger is in the register position (laying along the side of the frame above the trigger guard.)

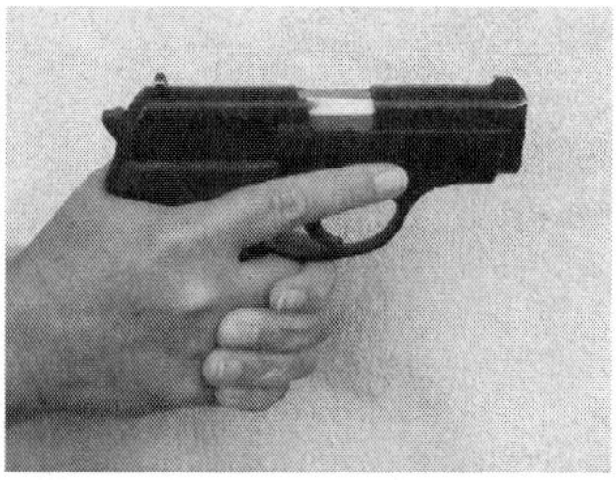

These photos show the trigger finger in the register position.

1. Explain to the shooter or establish that she knows the following components of the sight picture: eyes, front sight and rear sight aligned (with the front sight framed by the rear sight and with the front and rear sights level across the top) with the target.

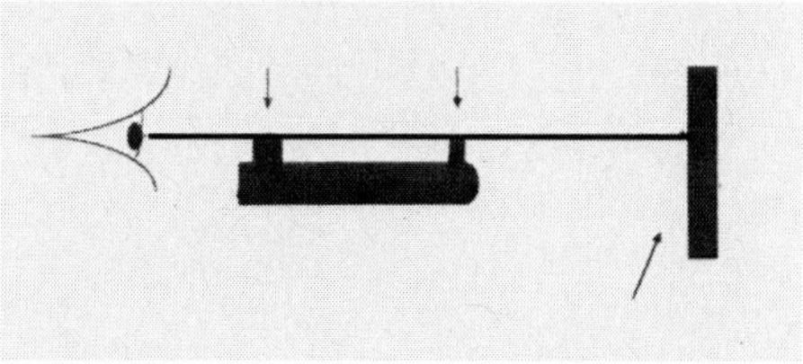

This illustrates the straight line between her eye, rear sight (left arrrow), front sight (middle arrow) and the target (right arrow).

2. When the gun is at eye level, the trigger finger must be in the register position (laying along the side of the frame above the trigger guard). The trigger finger only comes in contact with the trigger when the decision to fire the gun has been made and the sights are on target.

2. Explain that she must hold the front sight (framed by the rear sight) in the center of the target area *while* she presses the trigger. Tell her the front sight will be moving ever so slightly while she applies steady pressure to the trigger.

3. Explain that while she holds the front sight in the center of the target area nothing should move except her trigger finger. Her hands maintain consistent pressure on the grip. Use the word "press" as opposed to "squeeze" because "squeeze" may suggest that she contract her entire hand in order to press the trigger.

4. For multiple shots, she should continue holding the trigger to the rear of the trigger guard after firing until the front sight has returned to the center of the target after the recoil, then she should slowly release the pressure on the trigger until it moves far enough forward for the sear to re-engage. Once she feels and/or hears a click (catches the link), she would repeat the firing process.

5. In other words, the shooter is nothing but the launch platform for the gun. The gun does the work. The shooter holds it steady. You should describe all the steps completely so she knows exactly what she is to do.

Stance and grip are addressed in more detail in chapters 10 and 12.

Part II
Fundamentals of Shooting

Chapter 9
Safety

The ultimate goal of firearms instruction is for the student to master safe gunhandling skills and be able to consistently and accurately hit her target. Everyone who handles a firearm must always follow the basic safety rules. New shooters need to understand it takes concentration and practice to reliably apply gun safety rules. Experienced officers as well as novices must be watched while handling firearms. If a safety problem occurs, immediately stop the officer, explain what is wrong and how to correct it. Those who continually fail to follow safe gunhandling rules should be taken off the line for a review of the safety rules.

Students need to understand how to safely handle firearms before they start to work with them. After a presentation of gun safety rules, we make sure the student knows how the gun she will be using operates. We give her time to famialarize herself with the mechanics of the operating system. In many cases, this is the first time the student has ever touched a gun. Women usually ask more questions than men about how a gun works, unless they are made to feel stupid for asking "moronic questions."

Women who are given plenty of time to practice safety and mechanical skills become confident in their ability. We have found that the extra time for questions and repetitions at this point results in fewer problems in the future. This can be a challenge in a class with both male and female students because the males will typically want to "cut to the chase" and may become bored with too much detail.

Spatial relationships are an integral part of safe gun handling. The shooter must develop a specific awareness of where her gun is pointed. She must always be conscious of where her trigger finger is and what it is doing. The trigger finger is only placed on the trigger when the shooter's eye, front sight, rear sight and target are aligned and the shooter has made the decision to fire. Detailed instruction and demonstrations will help the shooter understand why it is crucial that she always knows where the gun is pointed and what her trigger finger is doing.

Here is an example of how important spatial relationships are to safe gun handling. A novice female shooter is on the firing line holding her gun down range when the instructor standing next to her asks her a question. She turns to look at him when she answers the question and her gun swings around with her body. The instructor grabs her to stop the gun from pointing at him.

She did not think about how her gun moves with her body. Her intention is to be safe when handling her gun, but her brain has not learned to automaticaly make the connection between her hand, wrist, arm or body movement and where the gun is pointed. She must develop a specific awareness of her gun -- where it is and what is in front of the muzzle.

We have yet to meet a shooter who was not concerned about safety. Some tell us that they are not sure they know how to safely handle their firearm in all situations. For example, they are afraid they will do something wrong when clearing a stoppage. We provide them with detailed instruction including a demonstration of what they are to do. Then we have them do a number of repetitions. This allows us to confirm that they understand how to safely clear a stoppage and it gives them confidence that they can do so without supervision.

Our objective is for the student to be able to demonstrate to us that she knows how to safely handle her gun. It is one thing for a student to be able to recite the four cardinal gun safety rules but the true measure of her knowledge is how she applies the rules.

The first rule of safe gun handling states that ALL firearms are always considered to be loaded and immediately ready to fire all the time. Unloaded guns are handled no differently than loaded ones. Too many fatal accidents are the result of a loaded gun being mistaken for an "unloaded" gun. Officers who carelessly point an “empty” gun at themselves or others are immediately stopped. If this behavior continues, they are escorted off the range.

The second rule is that the muzzle of any firearm must not, at any time, be allowed to point in an unsafe direction. An unsafe direction includes any part of the shooter's body such as hands, arms or legs. The muzzle must not point in the direction of other students or instructors even for an instant.

A safe direction is any direction at which a gun is pointed and when the gun is discharged will contain the bullet without damage or injury to property or people. On a range, the backstop is a safe direction. Other ranges may have specific rules.

The person handling the gun is responsible for keeping the gun "pointed" in a safe direction. We encourage the shooter to think about where she can safely point her gun when it is in her hand. Away from the range, a safe direction depends on the surroundings. At home, a safe direction might be a large appliance such as a refrigerator or heavy wooden furniture. An interior wall generally will not stop bullets.

Often the student is so focused on learning a fundamental, she forgets where the gun is pointed. If a safety problem occurs, we immediately stop the shooter and tell her what she has done incorrectly. Instructors must be continually monitoring students and muzzles.

The third safety rule states that the trigger finger must be in register against the frame and above the trigger guard until/unless the sights are aligned on a target and the decision to fire has been made.

The common reaction of a novice picking up a firearm is to immediately put her finger on the trigger. After all, that is what she has seen thousands of times on television programs and movies. Also most people pick up or grasp objects with all their fingers. For example when we pick up a fork or screwdriver we usually do not keep one finger straight. This natural instinct must be overcome by mental focus and repetition.

The final rule is that when pointing a gun at a target, be sure the target has been identified and that the area around and behind it is clear and safe.

Other safety matters

As instructors, we are responsible for providing a safe environment both in the classroom and on the range. Anytime someone handles a firearm it must be pointed in a safe direction. On the range, the backstop is the safe direction, however it is difficult to establish a safe direction in a classroom. Therefore when training in a classroom, we only use plastic prop guns.

An academy student in the Rocky Mountain region was fatally shot in the back of the head during a classroom exercise using "dummy rounds" in functional guns. The dummy rounds looked exactly like live ammunition. Tragically a live round was mixed in and mistakenly loaded into one of the guns. The desks were arranged in rows. As a result, students handing guns were pointing them at the person sitting in front of them.

Eye and ear protection

Eye protection is mandatory on the range. We require eye

protection to wrap around the side to prevent an empty case ejected from another gun from lodging between the glasses and the shooter's face. Shooters must wear a baseball style hat or visor pulled low so that it will prevent cases from falling between their eyes and glasses.

Hearing protection is also required. Muff-style hearing protectors are quicker to take off and put back on than the foam type plugs that fit in the ear. When using foam ear plugs it is important that the shooter knows how to properly insert them. Pulling up on the ear helps to open the ear canal so that the plugs can be pushed in and make a tight seal. Ear muff cushions should be soft. They need to be checked periodically to ensure they are still soft and pliable so that they form a tight seal over eye glasses. On indoor ranges some shooters may need to wear both ear plugs and muffs. Electronic hearing protection reduces shooting noise but allows us to carry on conversations.

Ammunition control

It is the range master's responsibility to ensure that students use the correct ammunition for their firearm. It is possible to load 9mm ammunition in .40 caliber magazines and load a .40 caliber round in a .45ACP magazine. It is possible to load 20 gauge shells into a 12 gauge shotgun. The result can be disastrous.

When should the shooter place her finger on the trigger?

This question is important because during training we are building sound habits. Shooters need to know where their trigger finger belongs. The finger does not belong on the trigger just because the gun is in their hand.

We have chosen to address this issue of when the finger goes to the trigger in this chapter because we believe it should be the result of a diliberate decision. If the student learns to place her finger on the trigger as the result of a deliberate decision, then her finger will not be on the trigger until her sights are aligned with the target and her eye and she has decided to shoot. This eliminates having a finger on the trigger at any other time the gun is in her hand.

Emanuel Kapelsohn is Vice President of the International Association of Law Enforcement Firearms Instructors and is on the Police Marksman Association - National Advisory Board.

The following is Mr. Kapelsohn's response to the question: When should the shooter place her finger on the trigger?

"Some instructors advocate the rule, "on target, on trigger, off target, off trigger." The first place I heard this rule was when I taught at Gunsite under Jeff Cooper. The thing most current proponents of the "on target, on trigger" rule don't understand is that, by then-existing Gunsite doctrine, one never came "on target" until the decision to fire was made — until then, the pistol was kept in a 45-degrees downward "ready" position. Cooper actually felt this "ready" position could be more intimidating to an opponent than having the pistol pointed directly at him — as well as having other tactical advantages (unobstructed field of vision for situational control, etc.). In any event, the rule as used at the old ("orange") Gunsite had exactly the same effect as training shooters to stay out of the trigger guard until one is on target and the decision to fire is made — because one never came on target at Gunsite until the decision to fire was made."

Mr. Kapelsohn continues, "I have worked as an expert in numerous accidental discharge cases, including at least two — one just now concluded — in which the "on target, on trigger" rule has resulted in unintentional deaths. This rule is far too ambiguous (especially when not tied to the rest of the Gunsite training regimen, as it rarely ever is) and allows officers and others permission to put their fingers on the trigger whenever they are covering a suspect with muzzle pointed at any part of the suspect's body, even though they have NOT decided to fire and DO NOT YET WANT to fire. It simply isn't a good rule, in my view. There are too many situations in which a suspect must be covered with a gun pointed at him, even though the decision to fire has not yet been made. With very few imaginable exceptions, I strongly prefer the rule, 'Keep your finger outside the trigger guard until you are on target and have decided to fire.'"

John Farnam is President of Defense Training International, Inc.

The following is Mr. Farnam's response to the question: When should the shooter place her finger on the trigger?

"Emanuel Kapelsohn is absolutely correct! Our biggest problem with guns in law enforcement is accidental discharges, not missing bad guys, although both are significant issues. 'Finger in register until sights are on target and the decision to fire has been made,' is the only appropriate way to teach trigger management, in my opinion. Pointing guns at people with one's finger inside the trigger guard, in the absence of any definitive decision-making process with regard to whether or not shooting is appropriate at that particular moment, is a veritable invitation to disaster. As Emanuel pointed out, such disasters happen all the time. With correct policy, reflected in correct training, the vast majority of them are preventable. We never seem to have time to train, but we always find the time to litigate."

Chapter 10
Stance

In general, women have less upper body strength than men and tire more quickly when holding a gun at arm's length. As they tire, they lean back from the waist trying to counter balance the weight of the gun. Accuracy diminishes as she becomes fatigued and her stance deteriorates. She loses her mental focus as she struggles to keep the gun up at eye level. She also tends to jerk the trigger in an attempt to get the shooting drill or qualification over with as quickly as possible so she can lower the gun.

The following exercise simulates what a small statured person or someone with little upper body strength experiences when they are holding a fully loaded handgun at eye level.

Standing up straight, hold an object weighing between 3 and 5 lbs at arms length with your elbows locked. Observe how long you can stand there before you begin to feel a burning sensation in your arm muscles, then your shoulders and finally your lower back.

The time it takes for fatigue to set in will vary from one individual to another. Even those in good physical shape will eventually get tired. Once you feel the fatigue in your arms, shoulders and back, bend your elbows so that the object is closer to your upper body. Does this relieve some of the fatigue? Now try to determine how long you can hold the object using the Weaver stance.

Once again fatigue will set in and you will want to shift your weight by moving your feet. You may find that you are starting to bend backwards from your waist.

These photos illustrate an exercise we do in our course for male instructors. We use sponges to increase the size of the grip and we add weight with a bag containing boxes of ammunition. After standing with the gun at eye level for awhile, their stance changes to compensate for the weight. We have them shoot several rounds before they lower the gun. This technique allows men to experience what many woman feel when they try to keep their gun at eye level for even short periods of time. The instructors also learn to appreciate how important the fit of the gun is to a shooter's ability to consistently hit the target.

Why we teach the Weaver stance

The Weaver stance works well because it brings the gun in closer to the body. If the weight of the gun is kept closer to the body with the arms bent, muscle fatigue develops more slowly than when the gun is held away from the body with the arms fully extended as in the Isosceles stance. Our goal is to reduce muscle fatigue in the lower back, shoulders and arms.

The Weaver stance works well even if the shooter wears a ballistic vest. An officer with a fuller bust may find this stance awkward at first and may need additional time practicing. We suggest practicing with an unloaded gun in front of a mirror. The benefit of reduced muscle fatigue in the arms and shoulders often motivates a shooter to master the Weaver stance.

The Weaver stance. Notice how the head is facing the target and the body is rotated. Her strong arm is slightly bent and the elbow on her weak side is pointing down. The Weaver stance was first developed in the 1950's by Jack Weaver.

How we teach the Weaver stance

The shooter starts facing the target squarely with the gun in her strong hand. The strong-side foot drops back until the shooter's chest rotates thirty-five to forty-five degrees. The shooter keeps her head facing the target. Without rotating her chest, the shooter extends her strong arm, pointing it at the target until it almost locks. The shooter's weak hand wraps around her strong hand with the thumbs up. The weak hand pulls the strong hand in towards her strong-side shoulder. The strong-side elbow will be slightly bent. The weak-side elbow will be greatly bent and rotated so that it is pointed downward.

When the weak-side elbow is pointed down, the downward pressure will balance the upward pressure on the strong hand that is produced by the weapon's recoil. If the weak-side elbow points to the side, the balancing effect is lost. The strong-side elbow is kept slightly bent and acts as a shock absorber.

Strength issues

The lower back takes most of the stress when holding a weight out in front of the body. We encourage the shooter to improve her upper body and lower back muscles.

Handguns vary in weight from the lightweight titanium revolvers to the steel frame high capacity autoloaders. An officer with less upper body strength will be able to hold a polymer frame 9mm such as a Glock on target for a longer period of time than she would using a full size steel frame H&K USP in 45ACP.

Chapter 11
Fit

Think of what would happen if the seats in all the department's vehicles were set at a fixed distance half way between being all the way forward and all the way back. Officers with long legs would always feel cramped and those with short legs would have to sit on the edge of the seat to reach the gas and brake pedals. These officers can drive the vehicle, but they do not have the same control in an emergency situation as officers who "fit" the seat adjustment. Fortunately, most officials have come to realize their officers have different sized hands as well as different amounts of strength in their fingers and issue a variety of firearms.

The size of the handgun in relation to the size of the shooter's hand can help or hinder her in learning the fundamentals of shooting. Traditionally guns have been made to fit the average to large size male. On average, women have smaller hands than men and women often have thinner hands than men. Women may have long slender fingers allowing them to reach the trigger on larger guns. However, the shooter may no longer be able to manipulate the trigger after firing a couple of dozen shots due to muscle fatigue. Another problem seen with slender hands is a lack of strength to control recoil.

Women with shorter fingers may not be able to reach the decocking lever on some autoloading pistols. Shooters with short fingers may have to rotate their grip in order to reach the trigger. This can cause the slide to malfunction. A locked but angulated wrist may not provide the support needed for the recoil energy that moves the slide backwards and forwards. It is not a matter of the shooter having a limp wrist, but the fact that the bones in her forearm are not aligned with the slide. This type of malfunction can be more than an inconvenience. It can have dire consequences in a lethal force situation.

Shooters who must rotate their hand to reach the trigger will often readjust their grip after each shot. This increases the time between shots. An inconsistent grip also affects how consistently the shooter hits the target.

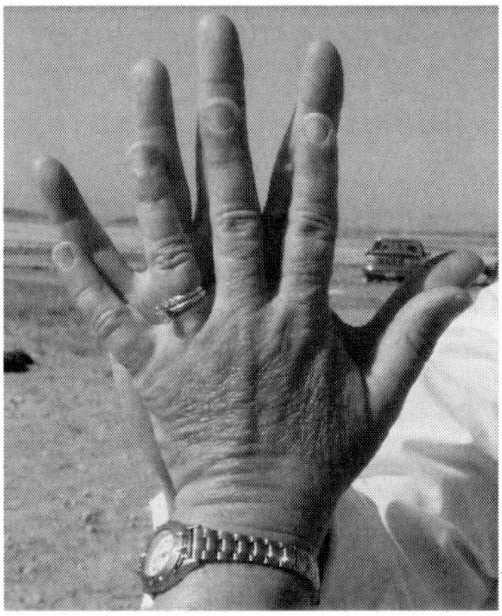

This photo shows Vicki's hand on top of a female student's hand.

The photo on the left shows a woman's hand on top of a man's.
The photo on the right shows a side view.

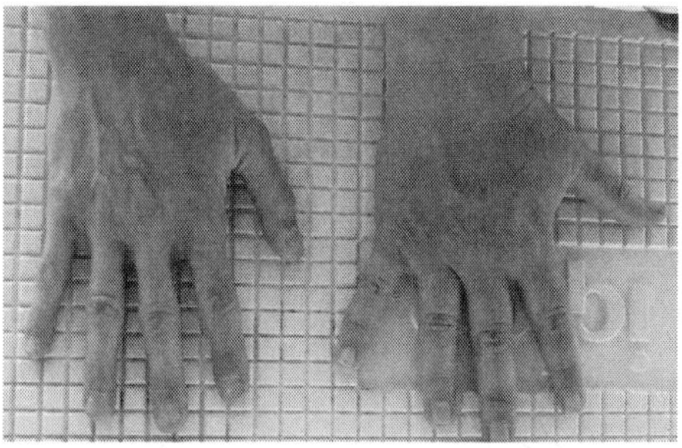

The woman's hand on the left has long, slender fingers and wrist. The woman's hand on the right is about the same size but has shorter, thicker fingers and wrist.

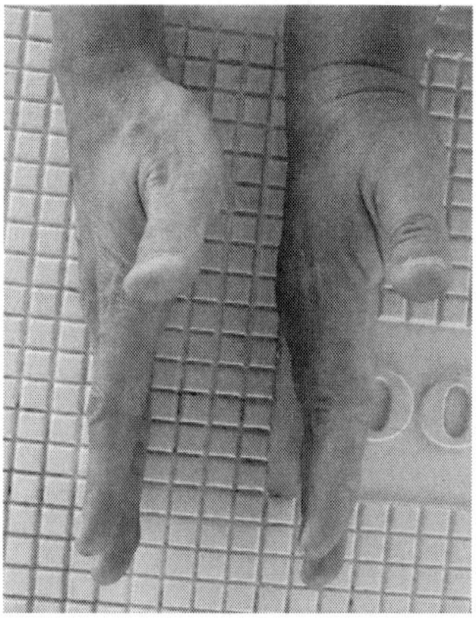

This is a side view of the same two hands shown above. Notice how much thinner the hand on the left is compared with the one on the right.

This photo shows a shooter with small hands gripping a gun that is too large. Notice how her hand is rotated towards the front of the gun so her palm is no longer behind the backstrap. Her wrist is locked but does not provide support for the recoil.

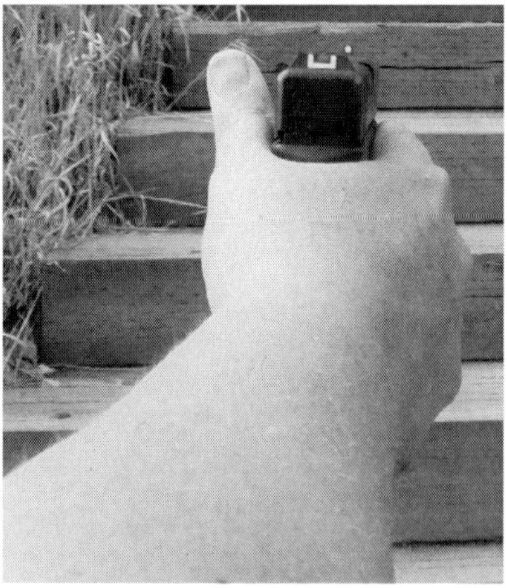

This photo shows a shooter gripping a gun that fits her hand. The barrel is aligned with her forearm and her palm is behind the backstrap.

The first thing we noticed as we watched Barbara shoot was her hits were sometimes low, sometimes high but always pulled to the right. Barbara is petite with rather small hands and was shooting a Beretta, the only gun her agency issued. She had been working on upper body strength so she was able to hold the pistol on target for a reasonable length of time. She had also been doing hand exercises so she did not struggle to press the trigger. However the size of the Beretta caused her to continually change her grip. In order to reach the trigger, she had to shift her hand around the right side of the grip so her forearm was not in line with the barrel. Sometimes she had the right thumb crossed over the left and other times the left thumb was on top of the right thumb.

Our first goal was to help her establish a consistent grip. We showed her the open space under her hands when she placed the left thumb over the right thumb. When she raised the right thumb so the left thumb could slide into place in front of it, the open space disappeared. This extra contact with the gun added stability. Barbara soon found this thumb position helped her maintain a consistent grip. Shooting with this grip improved her accuracy.

How the handgun should fit

A motivated officer can learn to accurately shoot a gun that is too large or a gun that is too small for her hand, but it will take focus and lots of time. A novice shooter will learn more quickly if she uses a gun that fits her hand, because it allows her to be consistent in how she grips the gun and where she places her trigger finger. Vicki has very small hands and, consequently, a lot of experience trying to find guns that fit. Here are some points to consider when working with officers who have small hands.

A handgun that fits well allows the shooter to reach the trigger without rotating her grip on the gun. The circumference of the grip should be small enough to allow the shooter to maintain a good grip with her support hand through recoil. Grips with finger grooves can also be a problem for women with smaller hands because the grooves are in the wrong position for a comfortable grip.

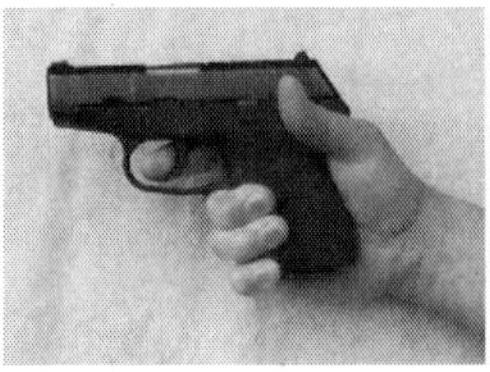

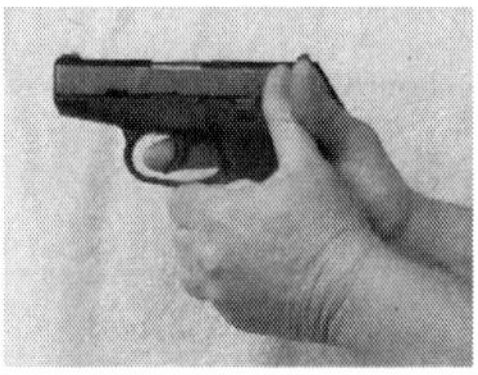

These photos are of a woman with very small hands. She is holding a small frame autoloading pistol. The photo on the left shows how her little finger does not fit on the grip. She can reach the trigger and still have her forearm aligned with the barrel.

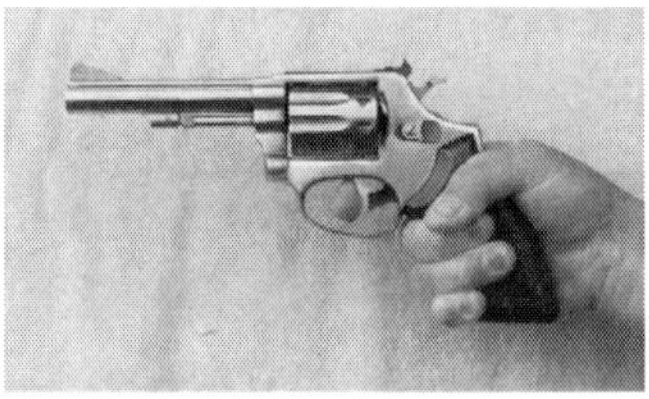

A woman with small hands is holding a large frame revolver on the left and a smaller frame revolver on the right. To reach the trigger on the large frame, she must rotate her hand. Very little of her palm is behind the backstrap.

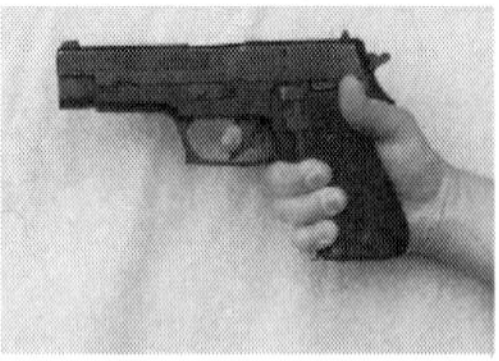

The photo on the left shows a woman with small hands using a proper grip on a gun that is too large for her. She can barely get the tip of her finger on the trigger. The photo on the right shows how far she must rotate her hand in order to reach the trigger.

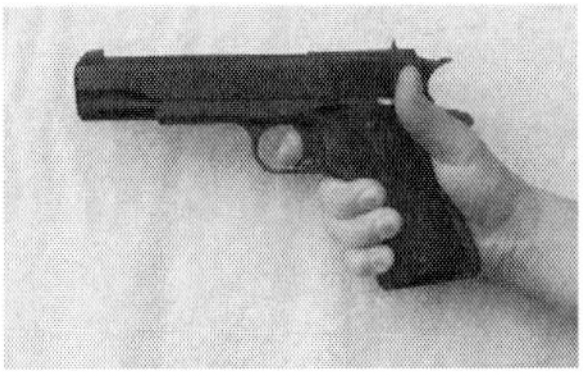

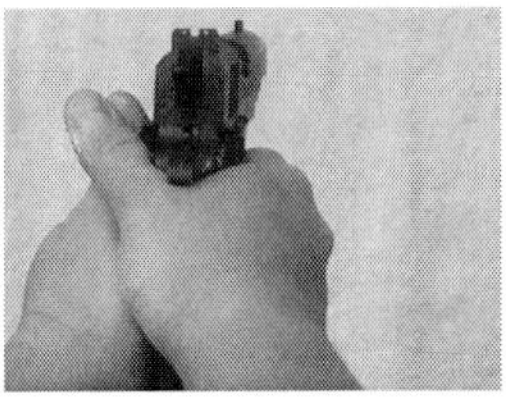

The photo on the left illustrates how a woman with small hands must grip the gun in order to reach the trigger. The photo on the right is a view from the rear. Notice how little of her hand is behind the backstrap.

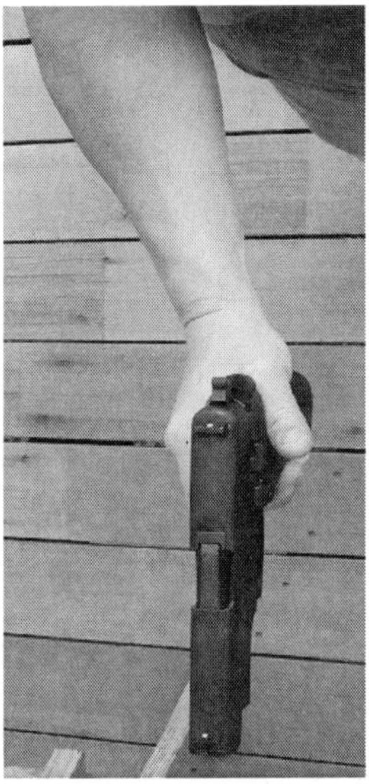

This photo is another view of the woman shown above. Her wrist is locked but she cannot position her arm directly behind the gun.

This photo shows how a woman with small hands is unable to reach the decocking lever. The only way for her to decock the gun is to change her grip, decock and then reposition her hand so she can reach the trigger.

Holsters

The overall length of a gun is a consideration for the draw because women tend to have shorter torsos than men. This means there is not much room between the grip of the gun and the woman's underarm. Many holsters will place the grip a few inches below a woman's underarm. When this happens, the officer will bend at the waist or to the side to "create" more room when drawing her gun.

This photo shows a female on the left and a male on the right. Her waist is several inches higher than his.

When a department reduced the time allowed to draw and fire six shots, all of their female officers (total of three) failed the drill. It took the officers so much time to get their guns out of their holsters that they could not fire fast enough to qualify. When in the holster, the grip of the gun almost reached their armpit. The officers had to bend to the side in order to create room to draw the gun from the holster. By the time they had the gun out and were standing up straight, they had used up most of the time allotted for the drill.

The best solution to these problems is to change the syle of holster. A low-rise holster will drop the grip of the gun down several inches so the shooter no longer has to bend to the side to draw her gun. If this is not possible, we teach the shooter to lift her shoulder and elbow straight up as high as necessary to gain a proper grip and clear the holster. This keeps her body upright, minimizes movement and is faster than bending from the waist.

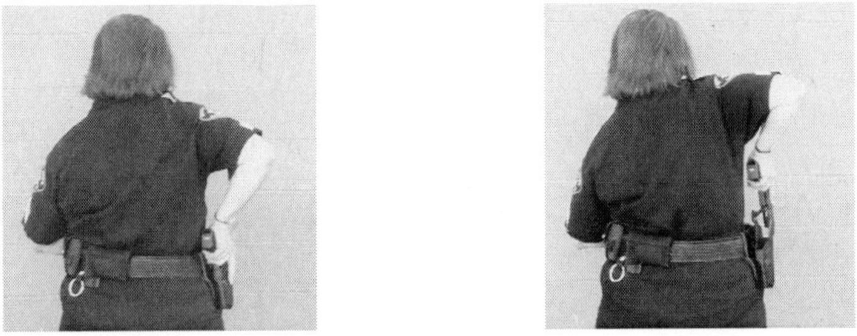

This officer is using a lower rise holster. The holster is designed so the gun is pointed straight up. This makes it easier to grip and draw.

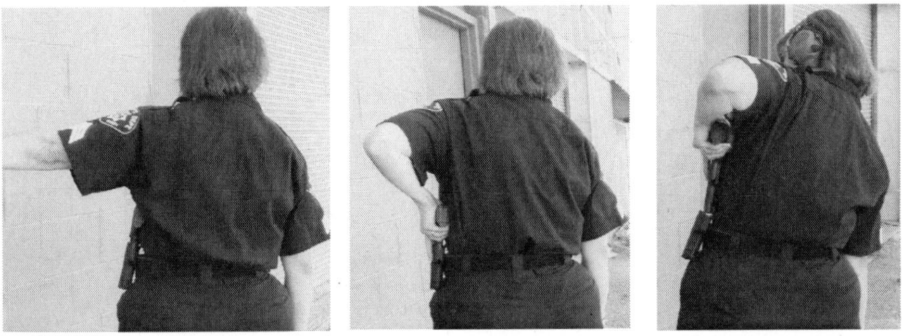

The photo on the left is of a standard holster. Its position on the officer's belt places the grip high and it also points the gun towards her body. The center and right photo show how far she must raise her arm in order to have the gun clear the holster.

Gun weight

A fully loaded double stack 45ACP weighs more than a single stack 45ACP. This difference in weight may play a role in how long the shooter can keep the gun at eye level. There may also be a trade off in how well a shooter with small hands can control recoil. A lighter gun may be more difficult to control than a heavier gun.

Chapter 12
Grip

Women typically have smaller hands, more slender fingers and less wrist strength than men. On average, men have larger hands and stronger wrists, which allow them to control larger, heavier guns for longer periods of time. Accurate shooting is not solely about brute strength, but strength does aid in holding the gun, aligning the sights, controlling the trigger and controlling the gun through recoil. The key to consistently accurate shooting is proper technique and equipment.

Acquiring the proper grip on any gun is a function of the size of the hand of the shooter and the size of the gun. The thickness of the grip and the reach to the trigger can cause most of the problems related to grip. Our goal is to teach officers how to achieve and maintain a consistent grip. It is vital she understands that once the grip is established, only the trigger finger will move when firing the gun.

To grip the handgun, the officer should place the grip of the gun in the web of her strong hand between the thumb and index finger. The barrel should line up with the bones in the forearm. The strong hand should be as high as possible on the back of the grip. The hand is snug against the tang on an autoloader. Both the strong hand and weak hand thumbs point up. The weak hand is placed as high as possible on the side of the gun and is wrapped around the strong hand so the index finger is wedged under the trigger guard. If the index finger is placed on the front of the trigger guard, it will shift position during recoil and must be repositioned after each shot.

The thumbs-up grip will often cause contact with the slide. This will not cause injury to the thumbs. The importance of the weak hand having as much contact as possible with the grip is often underestimated, especially for women whose hands are smaller than men's. The weak hand must be high on the side of the gun with the thumb up. This secure position provides support on the weak side and helps prevent the muzzle from moving low and left for right-handers or low and right for left-handers.

The left photo shows a good one hand grip. The photo on the right shows how the weak hand is high on the grip.

On a revolver, the strong hand should be as high as possible on the back strap without being in the way of the hammer. The weak hand is wrapped around the strong hand so the index finger is under the trigger guard. The thumbs will be crossed and may point down as long as they do not interfere with the trigger finger.

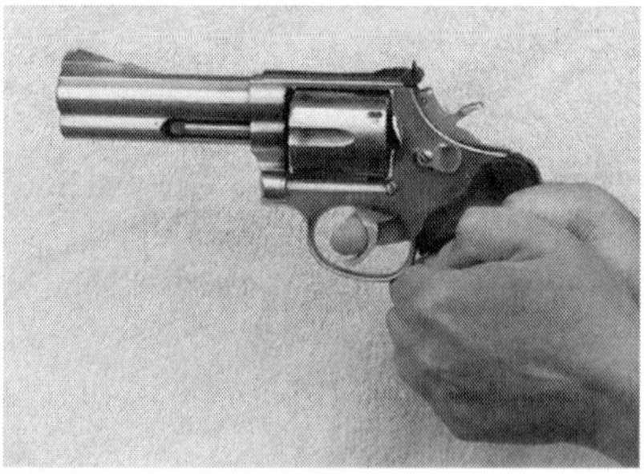

This photo shows a proper grip for a revolver. The thumbs are positioned over one another. This photo also illustrates good trigger finger placement for a revolver.

A low grip increases the amount of force placed on the wrist when the gun fires and increases the upward rotation of the muzzle. The upward movement of the muzzle during recoil can cause the wrist to break upward. In order to minimize readjusting her grip, the shooter should keep her wrist locked. It is important that the energy of the recoil be absorbed along the arm to the body.

This photo shows the thumbs up grip. It also illustrates a proper placement of the trigger finger.

On auto-loading pistols, the thumbs should point upwards and be parallel to one another. The weak hand fills in as much of the grip as possible. This hand must be positioned as high as possible to prevent it from slipping lower on the grip where it is of little use. The thumbs are kept pointed up and may make contact with the slide. This light contact is necessary and will not hurt the thumbs or interfere with the operation of the pistol. This position of the thumbs provides as much contact as possible for the palm of the hand with the pistol grip. It also provides support on the side opposite the strong hand.

Take care not to allow the shooter's thumbs to fall forward so that they interfere with the trigger finger or slide lock. If the thumb is under the slide lock when the gun fires, the knuckle can push the lever up and lock the slide to the rear. The trigger finger is in register (laying along the side of the frame above the trigger guard) until the decision is made to shoot.

The muscles, nerves and tendons of the hand work together. Sometimes new shooters and those with small hands may use a great deal of force to grip the gun because they fear it will fly out of their hands when it fires. If the pressure used to hold the gun is reduced from a death grip, they usually find that they have more flexibility in their trigger finger. Typically those with weak hands try to help their trigger finger by contracting the entire hand (a squeezing motion). Often you can see the muscle movement in her forearm as she fires. For right-handed shooters, the shot typically goes low and to the left. Left-handed shooters who contract their hand will probably end up with a miss to the lower right side of the target.

When the gun fires, a proper grip helps reduce the upward rotation of the muzzle during recoil and will allow the front sight to quickly settle back down on the target. If the hands separate during firing, the shooter must regain her grip, causing a longer shot to shot time. A consistent firm grip allows the officer to control the gun's recoil and helps decrease the time between shots.

What problems can be expected if the shooter has large hands and shoots a small frame gun? She may find there is not enough contact of her hand with the grip. For example, her little finger may not be able to fit on the grip. Accuracy diminishes as her little finger tries to grasp the grip and in that effort pulls the front sight down.

It may be difficult for the shooter to bend her trigger finger to avoid having too much finger on the trigger. Often her thumbs get in the way of pressing the trigger. It is difficult to maintain a consistent grip and trigger finger placement when the gun does not fit the shooter's hand.

Finger strengthening suggestions

Only a small percentage of women have strong hands and wrists. We encourage officers to develop trigger finger strength by using a squirt bottle. This allows them to establish a grip with their hand and only move the trigger finger. Avoid the exclusive use of exercises that contract the entire hand.

Problems and Solutions

Problem

An officer with small hands will have difficulty establishing a proper grip if the handgun is too big for her hands. When she holds the gun so that the barrel lines up with the bones in her forearm, she may be able to just touch the trigger or barely set the end of her finger across the trigger. She will not have adequate leverage to press the trigger so she will tire more quickly. These shooters tend to squeeze the grip with their entire hand as they try to press the trigger.

Accuracy diminishes because they will either push or pull the trigger to one side or the other, rather than pressing straight back as they apply pressure. If they squeeze with their entire hand, they can move the front sight low or high on the target. Shooters who try to press the trigger using just the tip of their index finger will involuntarily push sideways on the trigger. Shooters who manage to get the tip of their finger across the trigger will often pull sideways against the trigger as they try to keep their finger from sliding off. Either way, they add movement to the gun, which will move the front sight to one side. When faced with a time limit in which to make multiple shots, they contract their entire hand in a rapid jerking motion, never thinking to confirm their sight picture, but only wanting to get done in time.

Solution

The best solution is to switch the shooter to a gun that fits her hand. If this is not possible, try to make changes in the grip. Make it smaller and the reach to the trigger shorter, allowing the shooter to reach the trigger. Several manufacturers provide shorter triggers which decrease the reach to the trigger. The grip can also be adjusted using aftermarket grips. We recommend the grip reduction modification that Robar offers for Glocks. Another option might be to switch to a model of handgun that uses a single stack magazine, which is usually narrower than a double column magazine.

Sometimes the only solution is for the shooter to rotate her hand so she can achieve proper trigger finger placement. It is important to realize that when the grip is compromised, the reliability of the gun may be affected. If the barrel is no longer aligned with the bones in the shooter's arm the slide may not operate properly. The slide may not function if there is not enough support from the shooter's hand on the back strap. Either of these can cause a failure to eject or load. These malfunctions may not occur with every shot. It is important to understand that it is a lack of support rather than a limp wrist that creates a problem when the shooter rotates her hand in order to reach the trigger.

Problem

A shooter must learn to be consistent in the way she grips the gun. Often she is unaware that her weak hand changes position after every shot. She may switch from crossing her left thumb over the right to crossing the right thumb over the left. Her weak hand may creep forward as she shoots or the fingers of her weak hand may relax and then regrip with each shot. This lack of consistency will adversely affect accuracy and shot to shot time.

Solution

The shooter needs to understand that her job is minimizing the movement of the gun as she maintains proper sight alignment and presses the trigger. This means she must establish a good grip on the gun and maintain that grip so that only the trigger finger moves when firing. She must learn to be aware of what her body does. This takes a conscious effort at first. Given the noise and recoil, the novice or struggling shooter may not be able to tell how she is adding movement to the gun. One of the best ways to help the shooter learn what she is doing wrong is to mix snap caps into her magazine or cylinder. After each snap cap (malfunction) has been cleared and the next round loaded, stop her and ask her what she felt. Usually it will take several rounds before the shooter is able to tell how she is adding movement to the gun. It is important that she understands that it is her responsibility to continually monitor what she does with her body when she makes an accurate hit or she misses the target. There will not always be a range officer nearby to tell her why she missed.

Problem

The gun is too small for the officer's large hands.

Solution

The grip size can be increased by changing the grips. Some magazines come with an extension that increases the length of the grip. Another solution is to change to a model with a double column magazine.

Consistent grip for the draw

It is vital that the shooter learn to use a consistent grip when drawing from a holster. She should be able to draw the gun, bring it up on target and make an accurate shot without readjusting her hands. The strong hand grip should be established while the gun is still in the holster at the beginning of the draw. This allows her to control the gun while it is in her hands.

Chapter 13
Sight Alignment

The relationship between the rear sight, the front sight, the target and where the hole appears on the target is the key to proper sight alignment. This relationship can be explained by the following: wherever the front sight is on the target at the moment that the bullet leaves the muzzle is where the hole will appear on the target. The goal of the shooter is to hit the desired spot on the target. To do this, the shooter must minimize movement so the top of the front sight is aligned with the top of the rear sight with equal space on either side of the front sight while pressing the trigger. In other words, the shooter continually reconfirms the position of the front sight and makes adjustments as necessary while she presses the trigger.

We have found that a shooter sometimes considers lining up the sights and pressing the trigger to be two separate operations. First she concentrates on lining up the sights, then she allows her eye to move or focus on the target while she presses the trigger. As a result, she has no idea where her front sight was at the moment the gun fired.

While at a shooting conference, Vicki was confronted by a young woman who was looking for advice about improving her shooting skills. After a short discussion, Vicki reminded her that if she remembered nothing else from the conversation to remember this, "Align your sights and continue to align your sights while you press the trigger." The young woman looked puzzled and said, "But my instructor says to align the sights and then press the trigger. That is what I do. First I line up the sights, then forget about them and think about pressing the trigger." She was making two independent steps out of two processes which must be done simultaneously.

How we teach sight alignment

We start by explaining the relationship between where the front sight is when the gun fires and where the bullet will hit the target. For defensive firearms, with sights set for point of aim, point of impact, the result is always the same: wherever the front sight is pointed when the gun fires is where the bullet will hit. If the shooter adds movement, she may not hit the intended target.

There is a straight line from Vicki's eye, the rear sight, front sight and the target.

When the pistol is brought to eye level and pointed at the target, the shooter looks through the notch in the rear sight to the front sight. The blade of the front sight is positioned in the rear sight notch so there are equal amounts of light on each side of the front sight. Most people find their eyes will center the front sight in the notch without having to think about it. The top of the front sight is held even with the top of the rear sight so that together they form a straight line. If this alignment is held steady as the gun fires, the bullet will strike whatever is covered by the top of the front sight.

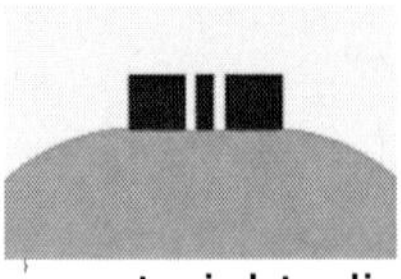

This drawing represents correct sight alignment when the shooter is looking at the sights. The top of the front sight is even with the top of the rear sight. The front sight is centered within the rear sight.

> *JoAnn told us she had been shooting for eight years before she understood sight alignment. Her instructors assumed that she knew and did not review the topic.*

We also present the shooter with a drawing where the front sight is higher than the rear sight and ask her where the round will hit the target. Then we show her a drawing with the front sight lower than the rear sight. It is sometimes helpful to hold a pistol in a proper grip and exaggerate having the front sight higher or lower than the rear sight so the shooter can see what happens to the muzzle.

We explain that our eyes can only focus at one distance at a time and therefore it is impossible to keep the sights and the target in focus at the same time. When the front sight is in sharp focus, the rear sight and target will be out of focus and appear blurred. An accurate hit occurs when the shooter concentrates on the front sight, keeping it aligned with the rear sight as pressure is applied to the trigger.

We remind the novice or struggling shooter there will always be some movement of the sights because humans cannot maintain a motionless sight picture. The sights will drift around the area of the center of the target. This drifting is normal and is usually not enough movement to cause a miss.

The shooter needs to understand she cannot spend too long acquiring a sight picture. The longer it takes to acquire a sight picture, the more possibility there is for the gun to move. After firing a shot, a consistent grip and stance helps bring the gun back into position quickly. When firing multiple shots, the officer has to make a conscious effort to not press the trigger too quickly or before the sights are realigned.

Dominant Eye

We have worked with more women than men whose dominant eye is not the same as their dominant hand. This is known as being cross-dominant (right-handed/left-eye dominant or left-handed/right-eye dominant). Handguns are held away from the body so it is easy for the shooter to shift the gun so the sights are in line with her dominant eye. The problem comes when she tries to fire a shotgun or rifle. With the gun mounted on the dominant hand shoulder, the shooter cannot align her dominant eye with the sights. The best solution is for her to switch shoulders. For example a right-handed but left-eye dominant shooter will need to switch to shooting with the left hand. This will allow the dominant eye to be aligned with the sights.

Here is a simple test to help a shooter determine which is her dominant eye. Using the dominant hand, point to an object across the room keeping both eyes open. First close the right eye, then open the right eye and close the left eye. The dominant eye will remain on the object. When the dominant eye is closed, the finger will appear to one side of the object.

Problems and Solutions

Problem

Often we find the struggling shooter has solved her accuracy problem by placing the front sight high and to the right of where she needs the rounds to go on a qualification target. She learned how to compensate for her trigger jerk or hand contraction rather than learning how to accurately put the rounds where she aims the front sight. This may go unnoticed for years in a department that always shoots on the same paper targets.

The shooter either discovered this "cure" on her own, another struggling shooter told her, or an instructor who did not know how to solve the shooter's problem told her. Very rarely will the shooter admit what she is doing. At some level, she knows this is cheating but it is a way to avoid the embarrassment and pain of failure.

Solution

A struggling shooter seldom volunteers this information so instructors may not realize what she is doing. On the range she may have a reasonable group at seven yards but as she moves further away, her hits will start to scatter across the target. We start by asking her to place an x on the spot on the target where she places her front sight. Another technique we use is to present her with a different target system such as steel plates. Her accuracy will diminish because she has to "guess" where to place the front sight in order to compensate for involuntarily moving the gun. We also find using a target with a printed camouflage pattern that does not allow her to see her hits is useful in diagnosing her accuracy problem.

Finally, we make sure she understands how her "cure" dooms her to utter failure when she is shooting to save her life.

Problem

We sometimes have a shooter who considers lining up her sights and pressing the trigger to be two separate operations. First she concentrates on lining up the sights, then she thinks about pressing the trigger. She has no idea what her front sight looks like at the moment the gun fires. She ends up watching the target rather than her front sight.

Solution

A good way to correct this problem is to tell her to continually reconfirm the position of the front sight and make adjustments if necessary as she presses the trigger. It is a continuous process with two parts - pressing the trigger and simultaneously confirming the alignment of the front sight.

Problem

A common scenario on the range is a shooter continually missing the center of the target, even though she swears the sights were aligned when the gun fired. We have to convince her the only way this happens is if the sights are off or that the front sight has moved.

Solution

We check to see that the sights are not loose or have moved to one side. Then we give her a target with a specific area marked where she should place her front sight. We ask her to take her time and make sure she brings the front sight back to the same place for each shot. After firing a few rounds, we go forward and look at the target. If the shots are not in the area marked for the front sight, we show her how the gun had to move in order for the front sight to be in the area where the rounds hit.

Snap cap drill

We explain to the shooter how using snap caps will help her "feel" how she is adding movement to the gun. We always show her what a snap cap is and how it works.

Load the officer's magazine mixing several snap caps with live ammunition. She may not notice what happens when the first snap cap goes into the chamber and she presses the trigger. We remind her to stay focused on what her hands and trigger finger are doing. After a magazine or two, most shooters begin to be able to tell when they add movement.

> *Snap caps have a brass base and a spring inside behind the area where a primer would be. When the firing pin hits the snap cap, the spring is depressed.*

Whenever the shooter has a successful shot, ask her to think about what she was doing with her hands and trigger finger and what she was thinking. During the snap cap drill, we make it a habit to ask the shooter where her hits are before walking forward to examine the target. In time, she should be able to tell us when she has missed or "thrown" a shot. At this point she is able to "self-correct" and no longer has to rely on someone else to tell her what to do in order to hit her desired target.

In our experience, most women find it easier to understand a spatial relationship by looking at a picture rather than listening to words. Words may not always create an accurate picture in her mind.

When the front and rear sights are properly aligned, the error the shooter might have will be in a straight line. The shot will land in the same place whether the shooter is seven or twenty-five yards away. This has been described as shooting through a pipe.

Improper sight alignment such as the front sight being higher than the rear sight will result in an angular error that gets worse with distance. From seven yards, the shot may be less than an inch above the center of the target. From twenty-five yards, the shot will be several inches above the center of the target. This has been described as shooting through a cone.

Chapter 14
Trigger Control

Any officer can have a perfect stance, grip and sight alignment, but still miss her target if she jerks the trigger. A controlled trigger press is a learned skill. For new or struggling shooters, it takes a conscious effort for them to control their muscles. These shooters must learn to manage what their body does. They already know from watching movies what to do to miss their target. Now they must break that pattern and establish a consistent routine. This includes a consistent grip, sight alignment, trigger press and follow through. Over time they will develop muscle memory and it will not take such a conscious effort to smoothly press the trigger. However, under stress, their mind will often focus on other things and old habits will take over. As soon as possible, they need to learn to sense and control their muscles. Just as importantly, they need to monitor their mental focus.

We use the term "press" because it provides the mental image of the index finger doing a task such as pressing the shutter button on a camera. We find the mental image produced by the term "squeeze" is one of the entire hand squeezing a lemon or a tube of toothpaste. The idea we want the officer to have is maintaining a constant pressure on the grip with only the trigger finger moving to press the trigger.

Size and strength issues

The size of the shooter's hand and the fit of the gun affect trigger control and accuracy. The strength of the shooter's trigger finger can also have an effect on accuracy.

How we teach trigger control to novice or struggling shooters

We explain that our goal is minimizing the movement of the gun when the trigger is pressed. It is important that the officers understand no one can hold a pistol completely still, and there will always be a certain amount of movement of the gun and sights. We explain that if the movement is kept within the desired target area they will still be able to hit with some precision. In other words, even when their hands are shaky, they can still make accurate hits.

Correct placement of the finger on the trigger allows the shooter to press straight back on the trigger rather than pushing or pulling the trigger to one side. For autoloading pistols, the shooter lays her finger on the trigger so the middle of the pad between the tip of the finger and first joint is centered on the trigger. Double action revolvers and autoloading pistols with a double action only trigger or a double action first trigger pull typically require more pressure to complete the trigger press. The finger is pushed further across the trigger until the edge of the trigger presses into the first joint. This provides the leverage necessary for most double action revolvers or autoloaders.

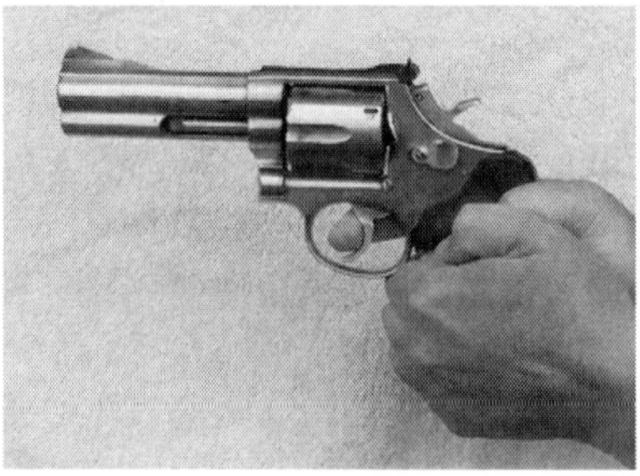

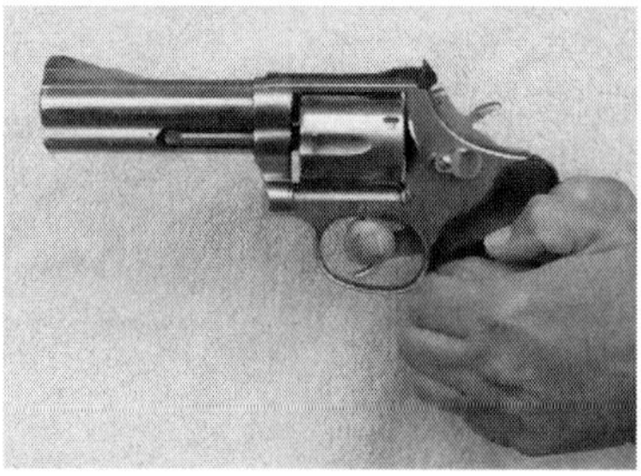

The photo on the left shows correct trigger finger placement for a revolver. The photo on the right shows too much finger on the trigger.

Press the trigger using a smooth continuous pressure. We demonstrate this and have the shooter take numerous dry-fire shots. Next we have the shooter bring the gun up to eye level and place a coin near the end of the muzzle and have her dry-fire. During this exercise, we encourage her to pay attention to what the muscles in her hands are doing. We remind her that during the trigger press, her eye is focused on the front sight to continually confirm proper alignment. Another way we demonstrate a smooth trigger press is to place our finger on top of the shooter's finger and press the trigger for her.

The left photo illustrates proper trigger finger placement for autoloading pistols. The photo on the right shows too much finger on the trigger.

It takes time to learn the muscle control necessary to reduce shot to shot times. A technique to dramatically improve accuracy and speed of multiple shots is continuous trigger contact. As soon as the shooter has a feel for what it takes to hit her target, it is time for her to learn how to keep her finger in contact with the trigger through recoil and how to reengage the sear (catch the link or reset the trigger).

Rather than allow the finger to fly off the trigger after the gun fires, the finger holds the trigger all the way to the rear during recoil. After the sights are aligned, the finger allows the trigger to move forward just enough to reengage the sear, then the trigger is pressed back for the next shot. The finger never loses contact with the trigger as the gun fires. This helps to minimize the distance the finger travels and it minimizes the movement of the gun. Hearing or feeling a click on some guns is more pronounced than others because some models have a very subtle click and/or short reset.

On revolvers, the trigger must return all the way forward after each shot due to the design of the internal firing mechanism. This is also true for some self-decocking autoloaders. The shot to shot time for these guns is inherently slower than with most autoloading pistols.

Continuous trigger contact and "catching the link" drill

We have the shooter dry fire, then hold the trigger to the rear while we manually cycle the slide. We tell the shooter to slowly release the pressure on the trigger allowing it to move forward until she hears or feels a "click," then presses the trigger back for the next shot. Repeat this several times until the shooter understands she does not have to let the trigger move all the way forward between shots.

> *With practice, a shooter can develop muscle memory regarding the distance the trigger travels to reset. Continuous trigger contact will become a habit.*

Problems and Solutions

Problem

As previously discussed, when a shooter with small hands grips a gun that is too large, she may barely be able to reach the trigger. Without proper trigger finger placement, she will push or pull against the trigger and cause the front sight to move to one side. We have found most of these shooters will contract their entire hand because they do not have enough finger on the trigger to use leverage. This squeezing motion usually results in a low shot pulled to one side (to the left for righ-handed shooters and to the right for left-handed shooters). Squeezing the entire hand can also put pressure on the base of the grip and cause the shot to go high.

Solution

There are several ways to change the fit of a handgun. The grips can be changed to help increase or decrease the distance between the back strap and the trigger. Some manufacturers now offer a short trigger (reduced travel). Another solution might be to change the model of handgun from one with a double column magazine to one with a single column magazine.

Problem

Yanking, jerking or slamming the trigger always moves the entire pistol just before discharge and results in a miss because the front sight has moved off target. We find most novice shooters yank the trigger back because it is what they have seen in the movies. Some shooters are afraid and jerk the trigger as fast as possible just to get the drill finished as quickly as possible. Also they may not understand the spatial relationship between the front sight, rear sight, their eye, the trigger, the target and the hole in the target. Every novice or struggling shooter we work with is surprised at how much mental and physical control it takes to make an accurate shot.

Solution

First we demonstrate a smooth, steady trigger press while taking a dry fire shot. We have the shooter practice this a few times, then go back to live fire and ask the shooter to pay attention to what the muscles in her hands are doing. During the drills, we explain how it is her responsibility to monitor what she is doing and to learn the difference between a trigger press and a trigger jerk.

Snap cap drill

We start by loading the officer's magazine mixing several snap caps with live ammunition. The drill works better when we vary how we load the magazine. For example, we will sometimes load two or three snap caps in a row. The shooter will probably not realize what happens when the first snap cap goes into the chamber so we remind her she needs to be focused on what her hands and trigger finger are doing. Soon she will be able to tell when she adds movement. Once the shooter has been through this exercise, we often find the threat of a snap cap magazine is enough to get her focused on her shooting.

> *We have noticed that women who struggle with the double action trigger pull of a revolver may pull the trigger 75% to the rear then get tired or relax, indexing past a loaded chamber. The shooter then wonders why she did not get all six shots fired. We explain how she skipped a live round by not completing the trigger press.*

Chapter 15
Recoil

Most shooters describe recoil as a push of energy against their hands and upper body when the gun fires, however this is only one part of the overall recoil experience. Other components include noise, control of the gun, recovery and reacquisition of the sight picture. A problem with any of these can reduce accuracy.

We find that the size and shape of a female officer's hands have an effect on how women perceive and manage recoil. A shooter with small hands using a gun that does not fit properly will take longer to regain control of the gun during recoil and return the front sight to the target. This shooter may lose whatever effective grip she had on the gun due to the force of the recoil and may have to reacquire the grip before shooting again. Recoil can jar a shooter's weak hand loose from the gun. In the worst case, lack of proper grip combined with recoil will cause both hands to be jarred loose. The shooter scrambles to reposition her grip to keep from dropping the gun.

The caliber of the gun can also affect how a shooter reacts to recoil. Even if she does not lose her grip and no readjustment is required, the gross movement of the barrel upward or muzzle flip will increase the time it takes for the front sight to return to the target. In general, smaller calibers have less muzzle movement than larger calibers. The amount of muzzle flip also depends on the relationship of the hand on the grip to the bore line. A proper grip as high as possible on the backstrap of the gun reduces the amount of pivot or upward movement of the muzzle. A low grip increases the upward movement of the muzzle. It is important to explain to her that she should not try to force the muzzle back down. Just let the recoil happen.

Another factor influencing accuracy is the amount of time allowed to make multiple shots. When there are no time limits, the shooter can recover from recoil and readjust her grip between shots. Shot to shot times will increase whenever she has to readjust her grip or deal with muzzle flip. The faster she tries to make multiple shots, the more effect there is on how accurately she hits the target. Accuracy decreases because she either shoots before acquiring the front sight on the target or jerks the trigger in order to get the shots off during whatever time limitation is demanded.

The more powerful calibers such as .40S&W, .45ACP and 357Mag may create recoil that is difficult to handle. The use of these calibers often leads to flinching or anticipation of the recoil by the shooter. Thin hands combined with sharp recoil can cause pain. The shooter flinches in anticipation of the pain. Internal bruising can occur after firing several magazines. The pain may result from repeated shooting over a day or two or it may be the result of damage to the ligaments of the forearm from repeated pounding of recoil over a period of months or years. Small hands, wrists and arms may succumb more quickly to pain than larger thicker hands despite the determination of the shooter. Wooden grips and exposed metal can also be punishing to small thin hands. Rubber grips help provide a cushion.

Although the 9mm and .38 Special have the most controllable recoil for most people, the recoil of these two calibers is dependent upon the frame material, gun model and the size of the shooter's hand. In general, an all-steel frame handgun produces less recoil than a polymer, aluminum or titanium frame. Most shooters find that a full size model produces less recoil than a compact model.

Some women can fire several magazines before their groups open up. A smaller statured woman shooting a large grip .45ACP may manage the recoil and have accurate hits for a number of shots before the effects of recoil start to accumulate. The slow recovery from recoil becomes more pronounced and her shoulders, arms and hands become fatigued. The usual result is that she starts mashing the trigger to get the next shot or shots over with as quickly as possible.

> *A former Army officer and paratrooper found a Glock 36 (.45ACP) fit her well, but after firing several magazines, her group started to open up. She has long, thin hands and the sharp recoil of the Glock caused her to develop a flinch after firing a number of rounds. When she tried a Colt Commander in 9mm, she was able to regularly fire over 100 rounds without flinching.*
>
> *Another officer used a 40 caliber handgun and had thin hands. She understood the fundamentals of shooting and the gun fit her well, but after firing two or three magazines, she started flinching. The flinch was in response to the pain caused by the sharp recoil. When she switched to a 9mm, she was able to complete a day on the range firing a couple of hundred rounds without flinching.*

We often find the .40S&W shooters do well at the start of a training session, but after a few magazines their performance decreases, especially if they have thin hands.

The tendons in the forearm can also experience pain if the grip is too large for the hand, causing the shooter to hang on tightly during recoil.

When Vicki switched from a 9mm to a .40 caliber handgun, she developed a pain in her arm between the wrist and elbow that slowly got worse. It reached the point where she had trouble picking up a glass of water. She was diagnosed with tendonitis of the muscle called the extensor carpi radialis brevis, the condition commonly known as tennis elbow. In Vicki's case, it was brought on by repetitive use. She increased the amount of force she used to grip the gun as she dealt with the increased recoil produced by the .40 caliber gun.

The doctor advised Vicki to rest her arm by not shooting and wear a disk to massage the area to relieve the pain. She was also given stretching and strengthening exercises to condition the muscles.

Noise and the startle response

Recoil produces both movement and noise. We have found that most women do not like loud, abrupt noises. Both happening at the same time can produce a startle effect in women (and some men too). This is a protective behavioral reaction that includes tightening of the muscles, changes in body stance and cardiovascular changes. A startle effect or reflex can become more pronounced if the person is already afraid or anxious. This may prevent some shooters from having as complete control during recoil as they need to have to be efficient.

We have had a few shooters who experience strong emotions when startled. For example, a shooter bursts into tears the first time she fires her gun because the noise is so disconcerting. The fact that the noise will not “hurt” her is of little significance since the reaction is involuntary. It may be necessary to have the shooter use both ear plugs and muffs. We have found that after the shooter fires several rounds, she learns what to expect when her gun fires and her startle reaction diminishes.

A visual component of a startle response can occur when a shooter is firing in low light conditions for the first time. We had a female student who was greatly startled by the ball of flame that shot out from the muzzle. She screamed that her gun was on fire! She thought the "fire" was coming right at her face. No one had ever explained how powder exiting the barrel continues to burn creating a ball of fire at the end of the muzzle. We told her how this happens every time the gun is fired, but is not seen in daylight or under bright lights.

Maria had only been shooting a few times with her boyfriend. She admitted to us that she was still scared of handguns. We soon learned that the loud abrupt noise of the gun firing startled her and caused her to flinch in anticipation. The movement of the gun did not seem to bother her. We had her use both ear plugs and muffs. This decreased the noise enough so that she was able to concentrate on controlling the trigger press and keeping the sights aligned.

Chapter 16
Follow-through

Some shooters are so anxious to see if they hit the target they often forget about follow-through. They look over the sights at the target just before, during or after they press the trigger. If the front sight moves before the bullet exits the barrel, the shot will be a miss. They must continue to maintain proper sight alignment and minimize the movement of the gun for the fraction of a second it takes for the gun to fire and the bullet to travel the length of the barrel and past the muzzle.

We have found that using a camouflaged target helps the shooter break her habit of immediately looking for her hit. It will take a conscious effort for her to keep her focus on the front sight.

Another common mistake shooters make when firing one shot is to relax prematurely. This can also happen with the last shot of a string. She knows she will not be firing again so she fails to follow-though. In a gunfight, you don't know that the shooting is over until the target is no longer a threat. And you can't know that before you fire a shot!

The shooter needs to be aware of how the sights were aligned when the gun fired. This will allow her to say where the bullet hit the target. Knowing how to call her shots will help the shooter to self-correct.

Chapter 17
Locking the Slide Open

Problem
A lack of upper body strength can also make it difficult for female officers to lock the slide back on an autoloading pistol.

Solution
We have found that the following technique works well. These instructions are for a right-handed shooter.

With the officer on line facing down range, have her draw the gun and point it down range. She must keep the muzzle pointed down range and keep her finger off the trigger and in the register position.

Keeping the gun pointed downrange, have the officer turn her body 90 degrees to the right.

Have the officer hold the gun close to her body for the best leverage.

Have her rotate the gun so that the ejection port is pointed down towards the ground.

Have the officer place her weak hand over the top of the slide as far back as possible making sure not to cover the ejection port. She is to grip the slide so that her thumb is lying parallel along the side of the slide.

The officer's strong hand is positioned on the gun so the thumb is underneath the slide lock lever. None of the fingers should be touching the trigger and the gun should still be pointed down range.

The officer pushes her hands together and past each other. Both hands push at the same time to utilize all of her upper body strength.

As the officer pushes her hands together, she should watch the notch that receives the slide lock lever. When the notch is above the slide lock lever, she pushes upward to lock the slide back.

This photo shows how the gun is positioned in front of the officer. The gun is rotated so the ejection port faces away from her body. Her hand does not cover the ejection port. She is pushing her hands together.

For the left-handed shooter

A left-handed shooter turns her body to the left. The ejection port will point upward. Her right hand will come over the top of the slide and she will lock the slide back using her right little finger to push the slide lock lever up.

We find that some female officers struggle with this procedure. Struggle is okay! The stiffer the recoil spring, the more difficulty she will have initially. We keep encouraging her and the break through of accomplishing it once usually leads to mastering the technique. Once she learns to lock the slide to the rear using this method, it will be relatively easy for her to learn to do it while facing down range with the gun in front of her.

Chapter 18
Speed

Although accuracy potential for females may be the same as for males, speed is less readily achieved. It will only result from numerous repetitions performed with smooth and efficient muscle movement. Once that is accomplished, speed will increase as long as the shooter has the motivation to make it so.

Speed of the draw

Holsters that are too tight or not supported properly can slow down the draw. When she has trouble getting her gun out of the holster, she will usually reach around with her weak hand to hold onto the holster as she draws the gun. This can be a safety problem if the hand lingers after the gun is drawn and is crossed by the muzzle. Also she may not always have the weak hand available to hold the holster.

Another factor that can slow the draw is when she has a short waist and finds the butt of the gun is only a few inches below her armpit. She will usually bend to the side trying to create enough room to draw the gun and clear her holster.

A low rise holster is the best solution to this problem. Some female officers have found a holster that stands away from their body makes it easier to draw their weapons.

Another problem occurs when the holster pushes the gun into the side of the female officer. This makes it difficult to grip the gun and she must push the gun away from her body in order to get the gun out of the holster. Having a holster that stands away from the body will allow a quick grip and draw. Some female officers like holsters that keep the gun perpendicular. Others prefer the gun to cant slightly to the front or rear.

Chapter 19
Learning Challenges Presented by Different Operating Systems

The fit, the caliber and the operating system are just a few of the items that affect how a novice or struggling shooter learns the fundamentals of shooting. A simple operating system is easier to learn than a complex one. For women with smaller hands and less strength, a slim 9mm with a light trigger pull will be easier to use than a larger frame .45ACP with a double action only trigger.

In this section we list a variety of handgun actions along with information about the size and trigger pull of each one.

"Double Action Only" Autoloaders (also known as "self-decocking")

This is a simple operating system which allows the shooter to become familiar with these handguns in a relatively short period of time.

Models with single column magazines are a superior choice for shooters with small hands. Models with double column magazines may be too wide and cause the shooter to rotate her grip excessively in order to reach the trigger.

The weight of the trigger pull can vary from 5 to 14 pounds depending on the model of the gun. Models with a short trigger pull can help the shooter minimize involuntary movement.

Proper fit can help improve the shooter's accuracy. A shooter using a handgun that is too large or too small will find it difficult to maintain a consistent grip and trigger finger placement.

Double Action Autoloaders With Single Stage Decocking Levers

This is a slightly more complicated operating system in that the shooter must learn to use a decocking lever. The shooter must learn to decock whenever she has finished firing and before the gun is lowered to a ready position or holstered. Additional time may also be required to achieve a consistent trigger press.

A model with a single column magazine will be a better choice for small hands. However the trigger is often further forward than on the double action only models and therefore smaller hands may have to be rotated around the grip towards the trigger in order for the trigger finger to reach the trigger. Models with double column magazines intensify this problem. Additionally, shooters with small hands and short thumbs can have difficulty reaching the decocking lever. The decocking lever should be operated with the strong thumb. Left-handed shooters often use their index finger to manipulate the decocking lever.

A long reach to the trigger combined with the heavy (usually 12 to 14 pounds) trigger pull required for the first shot with the double action autoloaders makes fit critical. The first shot may also take a long time to execute because of the length and weight of the trigger pull. Shooters with small hands may have difficulty holding the front sight steady while manipulating the long and heavy trigger pull. Shots fired consecutively after the first will not be so troublesome because the trigger is further to the rear and therefore easier to reach and the trigger weight is reduced (varying between 5 and 8 pounds).

Accuracy may be diminished due to the weight and length of pull for the first shot. This is especially true if the trigger finger is too short to reach the trigger. Another factor that affects accuracy is the necessity of holding the front sight steady for the length of time necessary to complete the first trigger pull.

Double Action Autoloaders With Two Stage Decocking Levers

This is the most complicated of all the operating systems. All of the previous statements apply with the addition that learning this operating system requires the further steps of manually depressing the decocking lever and, without pause, immediatelly pushing the decocking lever back up so that the gun will fire again as needed.

Single Action Autoloaders

This operating system includes a manual safety. The shooter will need time to learn to manipulate the safety using her strong thumb. The safety is taken off during the draw and put back on before lowering the gun to the ready position or holstering.

These handguns fit a wide variety of hand sizes because the reach to the trigger is relatively short. Shooters with small hands may have difficulty reaching and manipulating the manual safety with their strong thumb.

The trigger pull is short and light (usually between 3 and 7 pounds). This makes trigger manipulation easy and quick.

Accuracy is enhanced by the slim design and lighter trigger weight. In addition, the amount of time needed to make the shot is less and this means that the front sight does not have to be held steady for as long as with double action models.

Revolvers

Revolvers have a simple operating system that allows the shooter to learn how they work in a relatively short period of time.

Revolvers come in many different sizes of frames and the grips are easy to modify. This makes it easy to fit revolvers to a wide variety of hand sizes.

The length of the trigger pull and the weight of the trigger pull (from 10 to 16 pounds) can make it difficult for some shooters to fire numerous rounds even if the gun fits them properly.

Accuracy will diminish as the shooter becomes fatigued from the long, heavy trigger pull.

Chapter 20
Caliber and Accuracy

In general, a larger caliber handgun will produce more recoil and noise. An officer who feels overpowered shooting a larger caliber will end up flinching. This will result in a loss of accuracy and a dislike for the gun.

Calibers such as .40 S&W, .45ACP and 10mm can affect accuracy and performance because of their heavy recoil. This may mean that the shooter's grip is compromised with every shot. Recovery of the sight picture will be slower and thus increase the time between shots. Internal bruising is possible with heavier calibers such as .40 S&W or 10mm for hands that lack thickness or heavy bones. If the shooter feels pain every time the gun fires, she will not be able to stop her physical reaction. We find that switching from a wooden grip to a rubber one helps to cushion the shooter's hand.

Chapter 21
Rifle and Shotgun

The short, light trigger pull on a shotgun or rifle and the fact that the gun is braced against the shoulder helps to minimize movement. The distance between the front and rear sights (sight radius) is much greater than with handguns. This increased sight radius also helps to improve accuracy. However, these advantages only last as long as the shooter is able to keep the gun mounted. If the gun is too large and heavy for the shooter, she may only be able to fire one or two rounds before she is unable to keep the gun up.

Rifles

An increasing number of law enforcement agencies allow patrol officers to carry rifles. Popular models include the AR-15 or Mini 14 as well as .40 caliber carbines. There is minimal recoil with a .223 or carbine caliber and most women find that they can easily reach the trigger. Officers with less upper body strength can usually hold these rifles up for several shots. A petite officer may find that a rifle with an adjustable length stock is easier to use.

To accurately hit the target, the shooter needs to understand and practice the fundamentals of shooting: stance, grip, sight picture, sight alignment, trigger control and follow through. Even with the advantage of greater support from their body and a greater sight radius, shooters will still miss the target when they jerk the trigger or forend.

Shotgun

Most law enforcement agencies require their officers to qualify with a shotgun. For years, the policy has been to select one model that everyone in the department uses. This works well when most of the officers have a similar physical build. Height and weight restrictions are no longer a part of the hiring procedure and as a result an agency may have officers who range in size from barely five feet tall and less than a hundred pounds to over six feet, five inches and 270 pounds. The "one size fits all" shotgun may no longer work.

In this photo both shooters have shotguns that fit.

This officer is shooting a shotgun we use when we teach male instructors. We extend the stock with a slip on pad and add sponges so the shotgun is too large. It is more difficult to see the front sight and the gun does not feel balanced.

This officer is using a shotgun that is too small. He can still maintain his accuracy but will have to be aware of how close his right thumb is to his face and nose.

The fit of the shotgun is very important for several reasons. First of all, the shooter's eye acts as the rear sight. The shooter should be able to clearly see the bead above the muzzle when her cheek is placed against the stock. A shotgun that fits allows her to maintain a consistent relationship between her eye and the bead. Keeping her cheek firmly pressed against the stock allows her to move with the recoil and more quickly recover for the next shot.

When a stock is too long for a shooter she will usually be looking at the back of the receiver instead of the bead. She will have to lift her head off the stock in order to see the bead. If the cheek is not in contact with the stock when the gun fires, the recoil will slam the stock into the shooter's face.

The cheek should be in the center of the stock when the gun is properly mounted. If the shooter's cheek is closer to the back of the stock, the stock is too long. If she mounts the gun and her nose is close to or on top of her thumb, the stock is too short.

A petite officer who is firing a pump action shotgun that is too large may not be able to cycle the slide. The reach of her arm is too short to push the slide all the way forward. She may find there is not much strength left in her hand when her arm is fully extended. An autoloading shotgun will help but the shooter may still have problems seeing the front sight.

We always ask female shooters if there are metal or plastic tabs on the front of their bra strap. If these tabs are under the butt of the gun, they can cut the skin.

We have found that it is easier for men to locate their shoulder pocket than it is for women. Here is what we do for a right-handed shooter. We have her raise her right elbow above her shoulder, then feel for the indentation between her collarbone and shoulder joint. She may find it easier if she puts the fingers of her left hand under her armpit and uses her thumb to feel for the pocket. Once she has found the pocket, we have her hold the shotgun a few inches out in front of her body using both hands and bring it back into her shoulder. A slight shrug can help produce the pocket. We remind the shooter to pull the butt of the gun back into her body to help keep the butt in her shoulder pocket. We want to make sure the gun is not on the upper arm. The butt of the gun should not ride up above the shoulder.

We explain to the shooter how the shotgun and body should work together with the recoil by keeping the gun pulled into the shoulder pocket and keeping her cheek firmly pressed against the stock. Keeping the cheek firmly in contact with the stock helps keep the stock in the shoulder pocket. The shooter needs to keep her forward leg slightly bent and lean into the shotgun. The rear leg is straight. A shooter who has to struggle to keep the shotgun mounted will arch her back trying to cantilever the weight. The shooter will be off balance and could fall backwards when the gun fires.

Chapter 22
Remedial Training

In this section, we describe what we do when we meet for the first time with a female student who is struggling to become a competent shooter.

We introduce ourselves and let the officer know we are there to help her learn how to shoot to the best of her ability and we have high expectations of success. We explain that learning to shoot well takes time and effort on her part, but if she tries the techniques we suggest, she will see an improvement in her skill.

Firearms safety rules and gun handling skills are the first items we cover. We tell the shooter that if a safety problem occurs, we will immediately stop and discuss how to correct the problem. Next we inspect her handgun to make sure it functions properly. We also make sure the shooter understands how her gun works.

As we watch the shooter handle her firearm, we are evaluating her gun handling skills as well as her demeanor. For example, does she look confident or timid? Are her movements smooth or jerky? Is her body tense or relaxed? Does she look like an experienced gunman or a novice? This information helps us to determine what to focus on in the training session.

The next step is to look at how the gun fits the shooter's hand. If the gun does not fit, we will be watching to see if the shooter has difficulty maintaining a consistent grip while drawing and firing. We check to see if it is easy for the shooter's finger to reach the trigger while maintaining a proper grip. Can she reach the slide lock/release with her strong hand thumb? How far does she have to turn the gun in her hand to reach the magazine release button or the decocking lever?

The woman in these photos has fairly large hands. She is able to maintain a proper grip and trigger finger placement. She can also reach the decocking lever without changing her grip. Her thumbs touch the slide but do not interfere with its function. If she allows her thumbs to go forward, they will be in the way of her trigger finger.

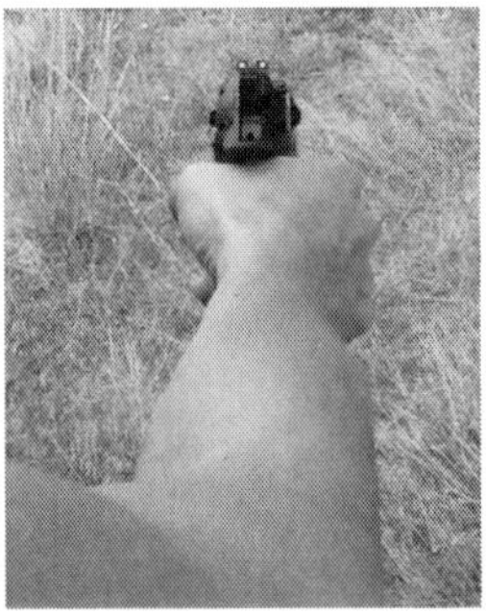

This is the same woman as pictured above using the same firearm. She is able to perfectly align her arm with the barrel of the gun.

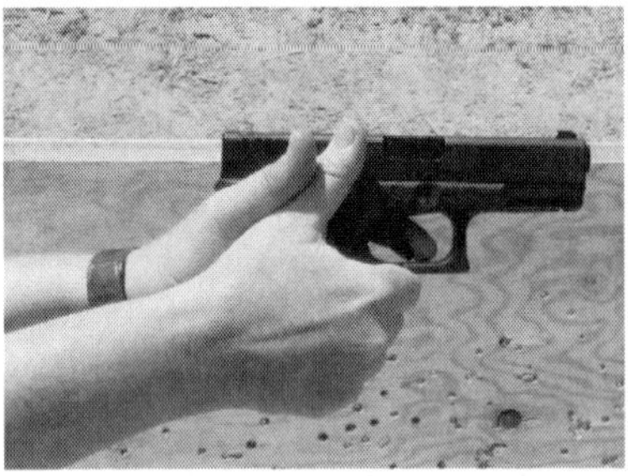

The photo on the left shows a woman with small hands using a small frame autoloader that fits her well. The photo on the right shows a woman who is left-handed. Again her gun fits her hand.

A smaller stature officer who is shooting a gun that is too big for her hands will have difficulty establishing a proper grip. When she holds the gun so that the barrel lines up with the bones in her forearm she is unable to reach the trigger with her index finger. If her hand is repositioned so that she is able to reach the trigger, her grip is compromised and she has less control of the gun. If only the tip of the index finger can reach the trigger, she usually does not have the strength for a smooth trigger press. What typically happens is she contracts her entire hand. A number of manufacturers now make models with a shorter reach to the trigger. Handguns with a single stack magazine usually have a less bulky grip. Whenever possible we switch the officer to a gun that fits. If this is not feasible, we try to replace the grip panels.

These photos show a woman with small hands holding three different autoloaders. The gun on the left has the largest frame and she can barely get her fingers around the grip. The one in the middle has a single column magazine that allows her to obtain a better grip. However she still must rotate her hand forward to reach the trigger. The gun on the right has a smaller frame and single column magazine. She does not have to rotate her hand as far forward to reach the trigger.

If the gun is too small for the officer's hands, she will usually wrap her index finger around the trigger. During rapid fire, the finger will slide across the trigger. Rather than pressing straight back on the trigger, she is pulling or pushing it to the side. This causes the front sight to move to the left or right. Depending on the size of the shooter's hands, changing the grips may solve the problem. Otherwise, we switch her to a handgun with a larger frame.

The stance the officer uses may be set by department policy or it may be left up to the individual. We have found that the Weaver stance works well for women because it brings the handgun in closer to their body. This allows the officer to hold her gun at eye level or at the ready position for longer periods of time. When she starts to lean back, it is usually a sign of fatigue. She is trying to cantilever the weight of the gun. We suggest that she work on building up the strength in her upper body and lower back. We want her to be standing upright, balanced on her feet and bringing the gun up to eye level.

Before we ask her to dry fire or live fire her gun, we confirm that she understands the relationship between her eye, rear sight, front sight and where the bullet hits the target. An easy way to start is to ask her to draw a picture of what her eye sees when her finger presses the trigger. We sometimes draw a sight picture with the front sight elevated or pushed to one side and ask her how this will effect where the bullet goes.

One of the best ways to help the struggling shooter understand what a good shot feels like is to do a dry fire drill. Most novice and struggling shooters find it easier to focus on what their body is doing without the noise and recoil of live fire. We have the officer load her gun with snap caps and take several dry fire shots. If she is using a self-decocking pistol, we manually cycle the slide to reset the trigger so that she maintains her grip.

Here is a list of questions to consider when watching a dry fire or live fire drill. How does she apply pressure to the trigger? Is it a smooth and continuous motion? Does she slow down, stop, then finish? Does she speed up at the end?

Often you will see the entire hand contract or the muscles in her forearm bulge. Most struggling shooters do not understand what a good trigger press feels like. They have no idea how much they are moving the gun.

When a shooter has a trigger control problem, we use her firearm to demonstrate a smooth steady trigger press then have her try it. If she still does not understand the motion, we do a dry fire exercise where we place our finger over hers and press the trigger while she concentrates on maintaining her sight alignment. We will also switch positions and hold the gun while she places her finger over ours and presses the trigger. A very effective technique that has been used for years is to place a coin on the barrel behind the front sight. The shooter is told that the object is to press the trigger without dislodging the coin. With practice, she should be able to complete several dry fire shots before the coin falls.

At this point we remind her that what we are looking for is consistency. We want her to maintain a consistent grip and only move her trigger finger while she confirms that the sights are aligned.

Whenever possible, we like to use steel targets because they allow us to watch the shooter and hear if she has hit the target or not. Steel also provides instant feedback to the shooter. Paper targets can be used to help diagnose a shooter's problem. Targets printed with a camouflage design are useful in training her to call her shots. These targets can also be used to help train her how to maintain her focus on the front sight and follow through when the gun fires rather than looking over the sights at the target.

During the live fire drill, we are looking for any movement in her body that can cause the front sight to move. Starting with the big picture, does her body move forward or back? Does she make a stabbing motion or bounce up on the balls of her feet or rock back on her heels? How does she handle the recoil?

Does she reposition her weak hand or adjust her grip after every shot? Is the trigger press smooth and steady? Is she blinking or closing her eyes when the gun fires?

After firing five rounds, we stop and ask her to tell us where she is placing the front sight of her gun on the target. This will help her start to develop her mental focus. If we have observed unnecessary movement, we tell her and ask her to start paying attention to what her body is doing. If necessary, we review the spatial relationship between the shooter's eye, rear sight, front sight and where the bullet hits the target. We ask her to fire several more shots and evaluate how she is doing.

In some cases, it is difficult to see the subtle movements she makes just before the gun fires. Mixing live rounds and snap caps in a magazine is one of the best ways to determine what she is doing that causes movement of the front sight. We explain that the snap caps will allow her to feel what her body is doing and that we are not trying to humiliate her.

Once she has successfully hit several targets in a row, we ask her to tell us what it felt like physically and mentally. We want her to learn to tell the difference between a good hit and a miss. If we are using paper targets, we ask her where the hits are before we go down range to look at the target. When we reach the target, we ask her to point to the spot where she put the front sight. Our goal is to have her start to feel the difference between an accurate shot and a miss.

We always try to end the training session with success. For some struggling shooters, getting three consecutive hits is a significant improvement. This small success may be the first positive experience she has had at the range. One of our goals is to have her believe that she can learn to shoot well.

A common scenario on the range is that a shooter continues to miss the center of the target even though she swears that the sights were aligned when the gun fired. We have to convince her that the only way this happens is if the sights are off (we test the sights to see if they are loose) or that the front sight has moved. We give her a target with a specific area marked where she should place her front sight. We ask her to take her time and make sure that she brings the front sight back to the same place for each shot. After a few rounds, we go forward and look at the target. If the shots are not in the area marked for the front sight, we show her how the gun had to move in order for the front sight to be in the area where the rounds hit.

Whenever she has a successful shot, we remind her to think about what she was doing with her hands, trigger finger and what she was thinking about. We make it a habit to ask her where her hits are before walking forward to examine the target. In time, she should be able to tell you when she has thrown a shot. At this point she will be able to "self-correct" and no longer has to rely on someone else to tell her what to do in order to hit where she aims.

Is it the shooter or the gun?

More often than not the struggling shooter will tell you that something must be wrong with the gun. It is easier to blame the equipment than accept that she is responsible for the poor shooting. However, sights do come loose so it is best to examine the firearm and then fire a few shots to check how well the sights work for you.

When asked to shoot a gun she is not familiar with, the officer will be mentally focused because she is not sure when the gun will fire. She is not familiar with the trigger pull so she pays close attention to what she is doing and may be surprised when the gun fires. The increased mental focus and the lack of ability in anticipating the recoil will help hold the front sight steady and thus produce a good hit.

Part III
Psychology of Shooting

Chapter 23
Responsibility

Learning the fundamentals of shooting occurs most efficiently when both the student and instructor are motivated to do their best. Those learning a new skill need to understand it is their responsibility to listen, ask questions, do their homework and participate in hands-on exercises. It is the instructor's responsibility to present the necessary information in a manner that encourages students to ask questions. The instructor is also responsible for determining if the student understands the fundamentals and is capable of consistently hitting the target without being coached.

The shooter is ultimately responsible for how well she handles her firearm and how accurately she hits the target. Our goal is for her to understand what she needs to do physically and mentally to make a good hit and to be able to correct herself if she misses.

Some officers never seem to take responsibility for their poor performance. They have found if they show up at the range, someone will coach them through the drill. Typically they are not mentally focused on what they are doing, they are just following directions, hoping to get a few hits and leave as quickly as possible. These officers will require intensive coaching every time they come to the range.

Academy instructors have told us that an increasing number of recruits are not seeking a career in law enforcement. These recruits choose law enforcement because of the benefits and work schedule. They stay for 4 or 5 years, often working in the department at night while they go to college during the day. Those who have a desk job have little interest in carrying a firearm or learning to shoot well.

Chapter 24
Mental Focus

The female officers we work with who fail to qualify or struggle to qualify usually do not understand the fundamentals of shooting. In the academy, many of these officers were able to mimic their instructors and fellow students. Most were able to qualify only when someone was standing next to them telling them exactly what to do. The bottom line is these officers do not know why they hit or miss the target.

Our first goal is to make sure the officer understands the fundamentals of shooting. Once she is able to accurately hit the target with several consecutive shots, it is time to start training her to develop her mental focus.

We start by asking her what she is thinking about when she presses the trigger. She needs to know she is responsible for hitting or missing the target. We can point out the obvious mistakes but she must learn what it takes both physically and mentally to accurately hit the target.

It is usually more difficult for people to concentrate if they are anxious. Officers need to learn how to concentrate on the sight alignment and trigger press regardless of the external and internal pressures they experience. The ability to tune out distractions is usually easier for men than women. The design of the female brain allows women to constantly observe the people around them - what they are saying, the tone of their voice, their body language, etc. Women are able to do several things at once, such as watch a security monitor and talk on the phone while they are entering data in a computer. Male brains are designed to concentrate on one specific task at a time. We do not mean that male officers will be focused on their front sight and trigger press and female officers will not. Rather this information points out the differences between male and female brains and why it may be easier for men to tune out external distractions.

Mental clutter

We find that men often have the same mental clutter as women. For example when we ask male and female shooters what they were thinking about when they shot a qualification course, they often say, "I was praying that I would pass." Other examples of mental clutter include: thinking about their past failures, thinking about who is watching them shoot or negative self-talk such as "I always miss from the 25 yard line."

These officers need to learn how to clear their mind and focus on confirming the alignment of their sights and controlling their muscles while pressing the trigger. Mentally they need to "see" the front sight and think about making an accurate shot. They need to stay in the present moment and focus on the task of hitting their target.

We encourage the shooter to be aware of mental changes that occur when she becomes tense. If she misses, we remind her to focus on the feel of a good shot. Both novice and struggling shooters are surprised at the amount of concentration needed to make an accurate shot.

Shooters can be distracted because they have impaired vision, their hearing protection is not adequate or they may be thinking too much about the mechanics of the shot. In some cases, a shooter will experience pain every time the gun fires and will not be able to control her reaction. It is best to stop the drill and determine what is causing the pain.

Good shooters often switch to "auto-pilot" and still do well. They have developed muscle memory and good shooting habits that allow them to perform even though they are not fully focused on the fundamentals of shooting. They understand the importance of these fundamentals and have practiced using them in order to be as consistently accurate as possible.

Pam had been a law enforcement officer for twelve years when she came to us because she was afraid of losing her job. She did not think she was getting the training she needed from her department. We started working with her and found that she did not understand some of the fundamentals of shooting. We showed her pictures of a proper sight alignment and talked about how easy it is to move the front sight when she jerked the trigger.

Using the snap cap drill, Pam learned to pay attention to what the muscles in her hands and arms were doing. Our next step was to help her learn to clear her mind and focus on the alignment of the front sight and controlling how she pressed the trigger. We also taught her the continuous trigger contact technique.

In just a few sessions, she had a breakthrough moment when she realized how much mental focus was needed to consistently make accurate shots. She finished a six shot string with a very tight group, smiled and said, "All I was doing was looking at the front sight and telling myself to listen for the click!"

The next time she qualified, she had the best score of her career. Pam is no longer satisfied to just pass the qualification and she continues to perfect her shooting skills.

Chapter 25
Coping with Anxiety and Performance Stress

"I will think of ways to break my arm so I won't have to go to the range. Then I think it would be too painful - but this is what I am thinking about in the days before I have to go out and shoot the qualification." It's not just the struggling or failing officers who have turned qualifications into monsters. Many officers find that when they step up to the line their hearts are racing and at the sound of the buzzer they yank the trigger as fast as they can.

Good shooters try to avoid excessive muscle tension but they do not assume that stress itself is an enemy. Shooters can learn to control stress by developing a positive mental attitude and by paying attention to what their body is doing. If the shooter thinks, "I always miss the target at the 25 yard line," most likely she will miss the target. We tell officers that none of the shooting fundamentals change at the 25 yard line. They must confirm the alignment of the front sight and press the trigger without adding movement to the gun. We encourage her to discipline herself to use the same technique for every shot.

When we see a shooter tensing up and missing, we suggest she step back, take a deep breath and try softer - not harder. We remind her to focus on what a good shot feels like. If she misses one or several shots in a row, we suggest she not dwell on it. She has to concentrate on the shot she is about to make and perhaps go through a mental check-list of the shooting fundamentals. Shooting is a skill that requires her to pay attention to what her body feels like.

A way to combat the fear of failure is to focus on success. We encourage shooters to behave and think positively. They should try to make every shot count and not think about their final score until they have finished shooting.

Ann is a sergeant who had always struggled to qualify. She explained that several weeks before the qualification she would start feeling very anxious. This anxiety continued to build so that she usually threw up just before going to the range. Once she was at the range, she had trouble aligning the sights because her hands shook so much. Mentally she was saying over and over "I hope I hit the target." She admitted that she was unaware of how she was interacting with the trigger.

We reviewed the fundamentals of shooting and found that she was not aware of the spatial relationship between her eye, the front sight, rear sight, the trigger and the hole in the target. She had developed the habit of slowly pressing the trigger most of the way to the rear, then finishing with a quick jerk. After firing a couple of magazines with snap caps mixed with live ammunition, she started to be able to feel what she was doing. We also taught her to keep continuous contact with the trigger. She was very motivated and her shooting quickly improved.

It took almost a year for Ann to change the way she reacted to the stress of qualifying. Changing her habit of becoming increasingly anxious about qualifying was a gradual process. As she became more confident and competent with her handgun, her anxiety started to diminish. Now when she goes to the range to qualify, she feels only a little stress. Her goal is to get a perfect score, not just pass the test.

Chapter 26
Motivation

It is very frustrating to set up special remedial range sessions only to find that the officers who need it most fail to show up. In this chapter we share what we have learned about why some officers avoid the range and what motivates others to seek help with their shooting problem.

Most people avoid painful experiences. For an officer who has failed, the range is the last place she wants to go. She is ashamed, embarrassed and feels humiliated by her failure. She hates going to the range for any reason and if there is a way to avoid remedial training or a qualification shoot, she will find it. Officers who are struggling to qualify will avoid any type of shooting practice until they are either given an order from their department or the stress of failure becomes so great that they finally ask for help.

Many of the struggling shooters we work with are motivated by the fear of losing their job if they continue to fail their weapons qualification. Some officers have come to us on their own, tired of failing and feeling that the remedial training provided by their agency is not helping.

Every so often, a promotion will motivate an officer to improve her shooting. A sergeant we worked with told us that when she was promoted, she realized none of the officers she managed had trouble passing their weapons qualifications. She had heard what they said about officers who failed or barely passed and she was determined to improve her shooting. Her goal was to shoot as well as, if not better than, the officers she supervised.

An officer being shot or killed motivates everyone to work on their firearms skills immediately after the incident. In most cases, however, this motivation decreases with the passage of time.

Some of the most challenging officers we work with are those who are not motivated and only come to the range under orders from their department. Many of these officers arrive with a chip on their shoulder. The shooter is usually angry that she has not been able to master firearms skills and the chip-on-the-shoulder attitude is a defense mechanism. In some cases, shooters with this attitude blame others for their shooting problem and have yet to take responsibility for their failure.

We find that motivated officers work hard and usually want to continue to improve their skills. The less motivated officers typically put forth the minimum effort necessary to avoid failure. They want to get the drill or test over with as quickly as possible and leave. Many of these officers are content to just barely pass the qualification and show no interest in improving their scores.

These struggling shooters may become dependent on the instructors' help, patience, interest, expertise and time. If this is allowed to continue, they will not be motivated to take responsibility for improving their shooting skills.

> *An example of this lack of motivation is a female officer who seems to forget her remedial training the next time she goes to the range. The instructor who worked with her became very frustrated because he had to keep reviewing the same material over and over again. It seemed the officer depended on the training staff to coach her through the qualifications. The first step to solve this problem is determining how well she understands the fundamentals of shooting. After reviewing the fundamentals, the next step is testing the officer's shooting skills. Once we establish that the officer can perform the necessary firearms skills, she must accept responsibility for her success or failure.*

A surprising number of female officers we work with have come to believe that they could never learn how to shoot well. This attitude can change if she learns how to correct her shooting problems and has the desire to do her best.

Melissa is a sergeant with over twelve years experience in law enforcement. She is a tactical defense instructor who trained at the FBI academy. Melissa came to us because she was struggling to pass her firearms qualification and did not feel she was getting the help she needed from her department. The first time we met with her, she asked us if we thought it was hopeless to try and teach her to shoot. What had happened to make her believe that she could not learn firearms skills? Melissa told us that she had come to doubt her ability to learn firearms skills after years of off-hand comments by instructors at the range. For example, "This is so easy anyone can do it with one hand tied behind their back." In other words, she had come to believe that there was something wrong with her which kept her from learning to shoot well.

We found Melissa did not understand the relationship between her eye, the front sight, rear sight, trigger press and the hole in the target. She was unaware of how she added movement to the gun by contracting her entire hand. Melissa did not have a consistent trigger press or finger placement on the trigger. When we asked her what she was thinking about when she was pressing the trigger, she said she was praying she hit the target.

The first thing we did was to assure her that she could learn to be an excellent shot.

Then we reviewed the fundamentals of shooting and started dry fire exercises to help her understand what her hands and trigger finger needed to do. We also taught her how to keep continuous contact with the trigger. During live fire sessions, we used lots of magazines loaded with live ammunition and snap caps. Several times during these drills, we would ask her what she was thinking about and remind her to focus on the front sight and what her body was doing. We tried to finish every training session with success. It did not take long before she was shooting fairly tight groups. The mental focus took a bit longer. Two years later Melissa was scoring well on her qualification and no longer felt panic at the thought of going to the range. She knows what to do to hit the target and she is able to refocus and correct herself when she misses.

Women in general want feedback regarding how they are doing. A thumbs up, smile or an excited "good shooting" are powerful tools to help develop motivation. Regardless of their level of motivation, we let them know we have high expectations of their ability to learn to shoot well. We remind them that once they understand and apply the fundamentals of shooting, the sky is the limit on how well they shoot.

It is not unusual for a struggling female officer to tell us she thinks shooting is difficult and she does not believe she will ever do well. She has set up a self-fulfilling prophecy of failure. This belief is reinforced if she knows her instructor has low expectations of her ability to improve.

Weapons qualification testing clearly identifies those who are struggling both to the officer and the trainer. Many times the shooter believes that she is incapable of learning to shoot well. If this is confirmed by the trainers' low expectations, it can set up and reinforce her failure.

A female officer who has been in law enforcement for over 20 years came to us because she wanted to improve her score. As we worked with her, she told us how angry she was with her firearms trainers. She said they were not professional and seemed more interested in showing off for each other rather than actually helping officers during remedial training. We helped her speed up her shot to shot time by keeping continuous contact with the trigger. After a few sessions, she was shooting more quickly and more accurately than before. The next time she shot the qualification, she did very well. Rather than continue to put up with the range officers' behavior, she gave up her gun for two years. She continued to shoot on her own at public ranges.

She recently moved to a new agency and found the atmosphere at the range to be very different. The instructors do not allow horseplay or joking around. Firearms training is treated as a serious business and officers are expected to work hard. Her job is more challenging because it requires frequent arrests of felons. She has become an excellent shot.

Negative Attitudes

It is a given that learning any new skill will involve a certain degree of indignities. Think about what happened the first time you tried to change a diaper, shave, hit a golf ball or break an egg. While learning to shoot, most people will feel clumsy or awkward and will easily become frustrated.

Many times a struggling female shooter becomes rigid and puts up a protective barrier that makes it very difficult for her to participate in any learning experience. It is not easy to break through this barrier because we all resist significant change. The effort has to come from the shooter. She has to suspend her disbelief in her ability to improve and abandon her dignity. In other words she has to acknowledge that she needs help and be willing to work to improve her skill. If she perceives that your intent is to help her rather than judge, embarrass or humiliate her, she will slowly learn to trust you and let down her guard.

Consistency of Instruction

As much as possible, we provide consistency in training by tracking a shooter's progress and avoid giving contradictory information.

Attitude of the range officer

Novice and struggling shooters tell us the attitude of the range officer plays a large part in either their success or failure. In general women are more sensitive to the tone of voice and facial expressions than men are. These officers will try to shoot with range officers who encourage them to do well. They say it is very difficult to keep trying when they sense that the range officer expects them to fail. In time, they can learn how to tune out this distraction.

Tears

Tears are often an involuntary reaction to fear, anxiety, humilation or frustration. When a shooter cries, we have her take a break to recover her composure and then resume our training. The less said about the tears the quicker she will regain emotional control.

Chapter 27
Courage

Courage is something that officers can develop. During a high stress situation, she will probably not become paralyzed by fear if she recognizes a task that has to be done and focuses all of her attention on doing it. Things are happening so fast there is not time to think of anything else but the task at hand. She can learn to be brave by practicing the skills she needs to deal with life-threatening situations. We encourage our students to practice using mental images to think themselves through incidents in which they are a survivor.

We reinforce the idea that firearms training is critical to the officer's job. We explain that when she is facing a lethal force threat, she should be able to quickly draw her gun, align the sights and shoot if necessary. She needs to think about the fact that in the line of duty she may have to take the life of another in order to preserve her own life or the lives of innocent people. Our training sessions are preparing her to act in a life or death situation. We know from studies of officer involved shootings that an officer will do what she has been trained to do even when she is scared. The only way to achieve this level of readiness is to practice. The same is true for other skills such as defensive driving or CPR.

Conclusion

In this book, we have presented a great deal of information for you to consider. We have made every effort to show you what problems women have on the range, explain to you why the problems occur and give you some remedies to correct those problems. None of this should be taken as a directive to give women "special" treatment. Rather, this book is directed at enhancing your skills as an instructor.

Women present challenges which were not seen when only males joined the police force. As we have emphasized over and over, these differences are significant. Women are usually smaller than men and most equipment is made for the average to large size male. Women learn more efficiently if given greater detail and longer amounts of time instead of minimal detail and short amounts of time, which suits men better. Women are more spontaneously emotional than men. All of these differences and no one has given instructors the information and skills you need to address the differences!

As instructors, it is our responsibility to understand who our students are and how best we can present material and skills which they can absorb and master. If they do not, we have not done our job thoroughly enough. Does this mean we will reach every single student? Certainly not, that would be unrealistic. But it does mean we must try to reach as many students as possible to the best of our ability. We, as instructors, must always be increasing our knowledge and skills to make our students as competent as they can be. Take what you find useful from this book and let us know what works and what doesn't work.

As Musashi said in the Book of Five Rings, "The instructor is the needle, the student is the thread."

Index